Grammar
with
Laughter

George Woolard

illustrated by Bill Stott

LTP
LANGUAGE

Language Teaching Publications

114a Church Road, Hove, BN3 2EB, England

Tel: 00 44 (1) 273 736344
Fax: 00 44 (1) 273 775361

ISBN 1 899396 01 2
© LTP 1999
Reprinted 1999

Copyright

Permission to Photocopy

The Author

George Woolard is an experienced ELT teacher and teacher trainer who has worked in Greece and Malaysia. He now teaches at Stevenson College, Edinburgh. His first book for LTP was the highly successful **Lessons with Laughter.**

The Illustrator

Bill Stott is a well known British cartoonist. His work has appeared in many magazines and newspapers. Sales of his books of cartoons exceed two million. He has spent the past 30 years teaching, drawing and living on Merseyside. He is a distinguished after-dinner speaker.

Acknowledgements

Cover design by Anna Macleod
Cartoons by Bill Stott
Printed in England by Commercial Colour Press, London E7

Introduction

Humour and motivation

Grammar with Laughter is a book which uses jokes to highlight grammatical patterns. Humorous learning materials have a number of advantages. Firstly, they increase motivation by being potentially amusing. Secondly, they are memorable and can help the learner to remember grammar. Lastly, they lead to spontaneous practice and consolidation of grammar through the learner's natural desire to share jokes with others.

82 worksheets

Grammar with Laughter is intended for intermediate students although the material will be of use to the pre- and the post-intermediate student. It consists of 82 worksheets to be used to provide supplementary grammar practice. The worksheets are organised grammatically, consisting of a series of jokes which have a single grammar focus. Each worksheet ends with a task which is designed to help the learner personalise the grammar focus item of the worksheet. This generally involves learners in producing information about themselves, their attitudes and opinions.

It is not intended that the worksheets be used to present grammar points. Once a class has completed a unit in their coursebook, the teacher can select the corresponding worksheet as humorous consolidation. Please note that some jokes appear more than once to illustrate different grammar points.

Some techniques

Here are some ideas about using the worksheets in class. There is no one set way of dealing with them. It depends on your students, your situation, and the kind of teacher you are!

1. Get students to do the exercise alone.
2. Get students to work in pairs to check their answers and decide on anything they did not understand.
3. Do the follow-up activity at the bottom of the page.
4. Get students to go back over the exercise, this time underlining all uses of the grammar point.
5. Ask students which jokes they did not find funny. Take a class vote on the best/worst joke on each sheet.
6. Cut up one (or more) pages and give each student one joke. They then have to learn the joke and tell it to another student without referring to the paper.
7. Give each student one joke to translate into their own language. Is it still funny?

Self-access

Grammar with Laughter is ideal for Self Access centres, providing a light but ideal partner to the many self-study grammar practice books that are available. Students can be encouraged to move from the practice exercises in these self-study books to the corresponding unit in **Grammar with Laughter.** Many of my students find this an enjoyable addition to their use of these self-study books.

George Woolard
Edinburgh 1999

Contents

Section One: Tenses

Lesson 1	The Present Simple
Lesson 2	The Present Continuous
Lesson 3	The Simple Past (regular verbs)
Lesson 4	The Simple Past (irregular verbs)
Lesson 5	The Past Continuous
Lesson 6	Past Simple / Continuous
Lesson 7	The Present Perfect 1
Lesson 8	The Present Perfect 2
Lesson 9	Present Perfect / Past Simple
Lesson 10	The Present Perfect Continuous
Lesson 11	The Past Perfect
Lesson 12	The Past Perfect Continuous
Lesson 13	Will / going to – 1
Lesson 14	Will / going to – 2
Lesson 15	Present used for future
Lesson 16	The Future Continuous
Lesson 17	Used to
Lesson 18	Have / have got
Lesson 19	The Imperative

Section Two: Modal Verbs

Lesson 20	Can / could – ability
Lesson 21	Can / could – requests
Lesson 22	Must / have to
Lesson 23	Mustn't / don't have to
Lesson 24	Must / can't
Lesson 25	Should / shouldn't
Lesson 26	Should have / shouldn't have

Section Three: Conditionals

Lesson 27	The First Conditional
Lesson 28	The Second Conditional
Lesson 29	The Third Conditional
Lesson 30	Wish / if only
Lesson 31	Unless / if not

Section Four: Passives

Lesson 32	Passives – present and past
Lesson 33	Passives – perfect
Lesson 34	Have something done

Section Five: Verb Patterns

Lesson 35   Verb + infinitive
Lesson 36   Verb + object + infinitive
Lesson 37   Verb + *-ing*
Lesson 38   Verb + preposition
Lesson 39   Verb + preposition + *-ing*
Lesson 40   Expressions + *-ing*
Lesson 41   Make / let

Section Six: Articles etc

Lesson 42   Some / any
Lesson 43   Much / many / a lot of
Lesson 44   A few / a little
Lesson 45   Some / any / no / every-
Lesson 46   Uncountable Nouns
Lesson 47   Possessives
Lesson 48   Reflexive Pronouns

Section Seven: Adjectives and Adverbs

Lesson 49   Adjectives ending in *-ed* / *-ing*
Lesson 50   Adjective + preposition
Lesson 51   Adjective + infinitive
Lesson 52   Too / enough
Lesson 53   Adverbs
Lesson 54   Adverbs of Frequency
Lesson 55   Order of Adjectives
Lesson 56   Comparatives
Lesson 57   As . . . . as . . . .
Lesson 58   Superlatives
Lesson 59   Comparison with *like*

Section Eight: Clauses

Lesson 60   Defining Relative Clauses
Lesson 61   Non-defining Relative Clauses
Lesson 62   Clauses with participles
Lesson 63   Noun Clauses
Lesson 64   So / because
Lesson 65   So + adjective + that
Lesson 66   Such + adjective + that

Section Nine: Questions and Reported Speech

Lesson 67   Reported Speech
Lesson 68   Do you know / Can you tell
Lesson 69   Question Tags
Lesson 70   So / neither / either
Lesson 71   What's your name?

Section Ten: Prepositions

Lesson 72   Prepositions of Place
Lesson 73   Prepositions of Direction
Lesson 74   Noun + preposition
Lesson 75   Phrases with prepositions
Lesson 76   Before / after / until
Lesson 77   For / during / while
Lesson 78   Phrasal Verbs

Section Eleven: Other Points

Lesson 79   Numbers
Lesson 80   Times and Dates
Lesson 81   Likes and Dislikes
Lesson 82   Requests with *would like*

Answer Key

Section One
Tenses

Tense in English

Tense is the way grammar expresses time through different verb forms. At least, that is what we normally think. Tense in English, however, is sometimes not directly related to time in the real world. The Present Simple can be used to talk about other times:

The future:	*We leave at six tomorrow morning.* (a plan)
The present:	*I take two eggs, beat them, then mix in the flour.* (a demonstration)
The past:	*So – just as we agreed – I ring her. I do my best to be nice to her. And what thanks do I get for it? Nothing! Just told never to ring again!* (a person telling a story)
All time:	*I love my wife.* (a statement which we hope will always be true!)

So, take care when you give rules to students about the tenses. Remember that it can be better to say nothing, rather than give a rule which is sometimes true and sometimes not.

Point of View

This is an important idea for students and can be helpful if you try to explain the difference between two tense forms, for example, the Past Simple and Present Perfect. You can look at the same event using both forms. For example:

> *I became a teacher 15 years ago.*
> *I've been a teacher for 15 years and I'm still enjoying my job!*

The Past Simple form looks at the event as a simple fact in the past whereas the Present Perfect form looks back on the event from a point of view in the present. You can see the link. That is why it is called the *Present* Perfect.

Sometimes the differences between two forms can be very small. It is always better to give more natural examples in context than try to give a rule, which is often only half-true and may confuse rather than help.

1   The Present Simple

Use *do, does, don't* or *doesn't* to complete the jokes:

1   What type of car . . . . your dad drive?
    > I . . . . know the name, but it starts with a "P".
    That's strange, our car starts with a key.

2   . . . . you ever have problems making up your mind?
    > Well, yes and no.

3   Dad, ... a dishwasher wash dishes?
    > Yes, Billy. That's right.
    And . . . . a bus driver drive buses?
    > Yes.
    And . . . . a weightlifter lift weights?
    > Yes. Why all the questions?
    Well, ... a shoplifter lift shops?

4   What . . . . ants take when they are ill?
    > I . . . . know.
    ANTibiotics!

5   What . . . . your father do for a living?
    > As little as possible!

6   What . . . . you clean your top teeth with?
    > A toothbrush, of course.
    And what . . . . you clean your bottom with?
    > The same.
    Really! I use paper!

7   . . . . you love me?
    > Of course, darling.
    But . . . . you love me with all your heart?
    > With all my heart, with all my liver, all my kidneys ...

8   . . . . this train go to York?
    > That's right, sir. Change at Leeds.
    What! I want my change here. I'm not waiting until Leeds.

9   Mrs Smith . . . . have soft and lovely hands like you, mummy. Why is that?
    > Because our servants do all the housework!

10 Mum, ... God go to the bathroom?
    > No, son, why . . . . you ask?
    Well, every morning dad goes to the bathroom, knocks on the door and shouts,
    "Oh God! Are you still in there?"

Using the following pattern, write similar true sentences about what you do often or regularly.
You could use the verbs *go, have, eat, drink, read, visit, buy* etc:
    I *brush* my teeth *three times a day*.
    I *visit* my parents *every Sunday*.
    I *wash* my hair *every two days*.

2 The Present Continuous

Use the following verbs to complete the jokes. Watch your spelling!

chew   *drown*   *eat*   *fly*   *give*
look   *tell*   *try*   *wait*   *use*

1   The police are . . . . ing for a man with one eye called Smith.
    > What's his other eye called?

2   Tell the passengers that I have both good news and bad news for them.
    > What's the good news?
    We are . . . . ing in perfect weather and we are making excellent time.
    > And what's the bad news?
    We're lost.

3   Is that your nose or are you just
    . . . . ing a banana?

4   It's Paul's first day at his new school.
    Excuse me, young man, but are you
    . . . . ing gum?
    > No, sir. I'm Paul Welsh.

5   Two sisters are in bed together.
    Are you asleep?
    > I'm not . . . . ing you.

6   Come out of the water. Swimming
    is not allowed here.
    > But I'm not swimming, officer. I'm
    . . . . ing!

7   What is the difference between a post box and an elephant?
    > I don't know.
    Well, I'm not . . . . ing you this letter to post!

8   A small boy is standing next to an escalator. He is looking at the handrail.
    Is there something wrong? asks a shop assistant.
    > No. I'm just . . . . ing for my chewing gum to come back.

9   A man is having a meal in a restaurant.
    Waiter. This meat is very tough. What is it?
    > The problem isn't the meat, sir. You're . . . . ing to eat the plate.

10   Why is your cat looking at me?
    > Probably because you're . . . . ing its bowl.

Please be quiet! I'm trying to listen to the radio.
Try to complete the following sentence in other suitable ways. Use the pattern:
Please be quiet! I'm trying to ...

3 The Simple Past (regular verbs)

Complete the jokes with one of the following:

always pulled	*smashed his false teeth*	*decided to leave*
didn't like her	*married the wrong man*	*worked as a Tax Inspector*
kissed her face	*ended*	

1   When I was a student I lived with a farmer and his wife. The first day I was there, one of the chickens died and we had chicken soup for dinner. The second day a sheep died and we had lamb chops. The following day a duck died and we had roast duck. The next day the farmer died, so I . . . .

2   At a show a very strong man squeezed an orange hard and then shouted to the audience: "I will give £30 to the person who can get any more juice out of this orange." Three very big men tried but none of them could get any more juice out of the orange. Then a thin, old man picked it up. When he squeezed it, five drops of juice dripped from it. The three big men were amazed and asked the old man:
> How did you do that?
I . . . . !

3   You're wearing your wedding ring on the wrong finger.
> I know. I . . . .

4   Do you know how my grandmother stopped my grandfather biting his fingernails?
She . . . . !

5   Mum, Aunt Sarah kissed me.
> Did you kiss her back?
Of course not,
I . . . .

6   Did the film have a happy ending?
> Well, everybody was happy when it . . . . !

7   My mother never liked any of my girlfriends. Last week I invited my latest girlfriend home. She looked like my mother, talked like my mother and even dressed like her.
> What did your mother think of her?
She liked her a lot.
> Well, that's the end of your problems!
Not quite. My father . . . . !

8   I think I was very ugly when I was a baby.
> Why do you think that?
Well, when I was in my pram my mother didn't push it, she . . . . it behind her!

Using regular verbs, write some sentences about what you did yesterday. For example:
  I *watched* football on television last night.
  I *walked* home yesterday instead of taking the bus.
  I *played* squash after work yesterday.

4   The Simple Past (irregular verbs)

Complete the jokes by using the past form of the verb (in brackets):

1   Why are you only wearing one glove? Did you lose one?
> No, I . . . . one. (*find*)

2   I woke up with toothache this morning, so I went to the dentist.
> Does your tooth still hurt?
I don't know. The dentist . . . . it. (*keep*)

3   The watch you . . . . me isn't working. (*sell*)
> But it was our best model.
I know.
> It was shockproof.
I know.
> And it was waterproof.
I know.
> So what happened to it?
It . . . . fire. (*catch*)

4   A little boy was in the garden and he . . . . a snake for the first time. (*see*)
He . . . . to his mother and said, "Come quick, mum. There's a tail without a body in the garden." (*run*)

5   Ronald got into trouble at the zoo yesterday.
> Really! What did he do?
He . . . . the monkeys. (*feed*)
> There's nothing wrong with that!
Oh yes, there is. He . . . .
them to the lions. (*feed*)

6   Mum . . . . a leg. Now dad can't work. (*break*)
> You mean your father is looking after your mum.
No, Mum . . . . dad's leg! (*break*)

7   My sister . . . . pepper in my face yesterday. (*throw*)
> That's terrible! What did you do?
I sneezed.

8   Student: I eated seven cakes at my birthday party.
Teacher: Don't you mean . . . . ? (*eat*)
Student: Okay, I eated eight cakes at the party.

9   I . . . . my dog yesterday. (*shoot*)
> Was it mad?
Well, it wasn't very happy about it.

10   A woman . . . . into a butcher's shop and pointed to a chicken in the window. (*go*)
> Is that the biggest chicken you've got?
No, Madam, the butcher . . . . (*say*)
The butcher . . . . the chicken into the back of his shop and . . . . it up with a bicycle pump. He returned to the shop and . . . . it to her. (*take, blow, give*)
She said:
> That's much better. And I'll take the other one as well.

Using irregular verbs, write some sentences about what you did last week. For example:
    I *read* a book by Charles Dickens last week.
    I *wrote* to an old friend. I *sent* her a photo of me with my new boyfriend.
Try to use: *saw, went, put, read, found, ate, drank, spoke, met, wrote.*

5 The Past Continuous

Complete the jokes by using *was, were, wasn't* or *weren't*:

1. You . . . . cheating at cards tonight.
   > But how did you know that I . . . . cheating?
   Because you . . . . playing with the cards I gave you.

2. A young man . . . . standing on a bus. He . . . . chewing gum. An old man . . . . sitting opposite him. After five minutes the old man shouted at him, "It's no good talking to me. I'm deaf."

3. A motorist was in court for speeding. He told the judge that on the day he . . . . driving at ten miles an hour and not at sixty miles an hour.
   > How can you be so sure that you . . . . travelling at sixty miles an hour?
   Because I . . . . going to the dentist at the time!

4. Mr Goldsmith . . . . shopping in an expensive London store. He . . . . talking to a young male shop assistant. "I want something unusual to give my beautiful eighteen-year-old daughter for her birthday." The young man thought for a second, then said, "Here's my phone number, sir!"

5. Two cannibals . . . . walking along the road when they saw a long line of people at a bus stop. One said to the other, "Oh, look, do you fancy a barbequeue?"

6. On the ferry to France a green-faced passenger . . . . leaning over the side of the boat. "Would you like your lunch out here, sir?" asked a steward from the ship's restaurant. The passenger . . . . feeling very well and said, "Just throw it over the side and save me the trouble."

7. Two very drunk men . . . . trying to find their way home, but they were lost. They . . . . staggering along a railway line. "This is a very long staircase," said the first one. "My legs are killing me!"
   The second drunk . . . .
   holding his back. "And the
   handrail is so low my back
   is killing me!"

8. John, what were you doing
   out there in the rain?
   > I . . . . getting wet, mum!

9. Two little boys were on holiday.
   They . . . . paddling in the sea.
   "Your feet are really dirty," one boy said
   to the other. "I know. We didn't come
   last year."

10. Mr and Mrs Smith . . . . arguing
    at the dinner table. After half an hour
    Mrs Smith said, "I've had enough. One
    more word out of you and I'm going
    back to live with my mother."
    Mr Smith looked at his wife and then shouted, "Taxi!"

Find out what some of your classmates *were doing* at seven o'clock last night.
   What were you doing at 7 o'clock last night?
Then work in pairs asking each other the following:
   What were you doing just before you left home today?
   Can you remember what you were doing when you heard of the death of Princess Diana?

6   Past Simple / Continuous

Complete the jokes below by using the correct tense of the verb in brackets:

1   Dad. What do you call a small brown thing with ten legs, and green eyes?
    > I don't know, son. Why do you ask?
    Well, one . . . . along your lettuce just before you . . . . it! *(crawl, eat)*

2   Harry . . . . a large grandfather clock on his shoulder. *(carry)* He was delivering
    it to a customer. He couldn't see what was on his right hand side and he . . . .
    over an old lady who . . . . in a shop window. *(knock, look)* "I'm very, very sorry,"
    said the man.
    "Idiot!" shouted the old woman. "Why can't you wear a watch like everybody else?"

3   What . . . . you . . . . in my apple tree last night, young man? *(do)*
    > Well, one of your apples . . . . down when I . . . . your garden so I
    . . . . it back for you! *(fall, pass, put)*

4   Magic Bob was a magician on a cruise ship. Each night he took objects from the
    passengers and made them disappear, then reappear in strange places. The captain of the
    ship had a parrot which always shouted "Rubbish!" at the end of the magician's act. One
    day the ship . . . . an iceberg and . . . . *(hit, sink)* The magician and the
    parrot were the only survivors. While they . . . . on a large piece of wood in the
    water, the parrot . . . . , *(lie, say)* "OK, genius. Where's the ship?"

5   A lifeguard . . . . a young lady the kiss of life
    when her husband . . . . *(give, arrive)*.
    > What are you doing to my wife?
    I'm giving her artificial respiration.
    > Artificial! Give her the real thing. I'll pay for it.

6   Doctor, lots of my hair . . . . . . out while
    I . . . . it this morning. *(fall, brush)*
    Have you got anything for it?
    > Sure. Here's a box.

7   A young man was in the
    middle of a road with his
    right ear to the ground.
    An old lady asked him:
    > What are you listening for?
    A motorbike passed this spot ten minutes ago.
    > That's incredible! How do you know that?
    Because it . . . . me while I . . . . the road and it . . . . my neck!
    (hit, cross, break)

8   How did you get that big red lump on your nose?
    > I . . . . a brose while I . . . . in the garden. *(smell, work)*
    But there is no 'b' in rose.
    > There was in this one!

Talk or write about accidents you had, while you were doing something else. For example:
    I *cut (past simple)* my hand badly while I *was peeling (past continuous)* some potatoes.
    I *scraped* the side of my car while I *was parking* in town.

7 The Present Perfect 1

Complete the jokes by using the correct form of the verb in brackets:

1 Doctor, I'm very nervous. This is the first time I've ever .... an operation. *(need)*
> Don't worry, I feel the same. This is the first operation I've ever .... *(perform)*

2 A famous film star went into a shop in a small town.
> Haven't I .... you somewhere before? said the shop assistant. *(see)*
In the cinema, perhaps? said the film star with a smile.
> Maybe. Where do you usually sit?

3 Hairdresser: I've .... a lot of strange
                  customers in my time. *(have)*
   Customer: Have you ever .... a
                  man with a wooden leg? *(shave)*
   Hairdresser: No. I always use a razor.

4 What are you fishing for?
> Mumamamamoolays.
What do they look like?
> I don't know. I've never ....
one. *(catch)*

5 Have you ever .... in the hot
sun? *(swim)*
> Don't be stupid. I only swim in the sea.

6 What do you do?
> I'm a sailor.
Have you ever .... on a
submarine? *(work)*
> No. I can't sleep with the windows closed.

7 It was my husband's birthday yesterday and he said,
Take me somewhere I've never .... before. *(be)*
> So where did you take him?
Into the kitchen!

8 Have you ever .... from a really bad headache? *(suffer)*
> Yes, quite often.
What do you do about them?
> I stick my head through a window and the pane disappears!

9 Dr Findlay was passing one of his patients in the street.
Hello, Mrs Merton. You haven't .... me for ages. *(visit)*
> I know, doctor. I've been ill.

10 This is a very good coat. It is made from the best wool.
> Can I wear it in wet weather?
Of course, madam. Have you ever .... across a sheep with an umbrella? *(come)*

Write down some sentences about yourself beginning *I've never ...* . For example:
   I've never flown on Concorde.   I've never been to Disneyland.
   I've never told a lie in my life.   I've never learned to drive.

8   The Present Perfect 2

Complete these jokes by using the Present Perfect of the verb in brackets:

1 Baby snake: Are we poisonous?
     Mother snake: Yes, we are. Why do you ask?
     Baby snake: Because I . . . . just . . . . my tongue. *(bite)*

2 You . . . . your shoes on the wrong feet. *(put)*
     > But these are the only feet I have.

3 Doctor, my son . . . . a bullet.
     (swallow)
     > Well, don't point him at me!

4 What's wrong, son?
     > I . . . . . just . . . . a fight
     with your wife! *(have)*

5 Waiter! What is this?
     > It's bean soup.
     I don't care what it . . . .
     (be) I want to know what it is now.

6 Mrs Millar went into a department store to buy a new dress. At first she wanted a long
     dress, then she wanted a short one. After an hour she said to the shop assistant,
     I . . . . my mind again. *(change)*
     > And does the new one work any better? replied the irritated shop assistant.

7 Dad, I . . . . to become a train driver. *(decide)*
     > Well, son, I certainly won't stand in your way.

8 British scientists . . . . a robot doctor. *(invent)*
     > Really! What does it operate on?
     Batteries, I think.

9 Hi, everybody! I . . . . the chicken soup. *(make)*
     > What a relief, whispered Andrew.
     I thought it was for us!

10 Ladies and gentlemen, this is your captain speaking. I'm sorry to announce that one of
     our engines . . . . *(stop)*. This means that the flight will be about 20 minutes late.
     (Ten minutes later)
     This is your captain again. I'm afraid another engine . . . . *(stop)* This means
     that the flight will now land 40 minutes late. Please accept our apologies.
     A little old lady turned to the young man beside her and said:
     > I hope the other engine doesn't stop or we'll be up here all night!

Underline all the verbs in the jokes which are regular.
**Make up some sentences about what you *have done* today. For example: *I've washed the
dishes twice today.***

9 Present Perfect / Past Simple

Using the Present Perfect or the Past Simple, complete the following jokes:

1   . . . . you . . . . *(be)* to America before?
    > No. This is my first time.
    Did you know that Christopher Columbus . . . . *(find)* America?
    > Really? I never knew it was lost!

2   When you . . . . *(sell)* me this car this morning, you . . . . *(say)* it was
    trouble-free. Since then, the brakes . . . . *(fail)* and the door . . . . *(fall)* off.
    > Well, sir, I did sell you the car but the trouble was free!

3   Doctor, I . . . . *(have)* a sore stomach ever since I . . . . . . *(eat)* three crabs last week.
    > . . . . . . they . . . . *(smell)* bad when you . . . . *(take)* them out of their shells?
    What do you mean – took them out of their shells?

4   Now, ... everyone . . . . *(read)* the chapter on Lord Nelson for homework?
    > Yes, sir.
    Kevin, in which battle . . . . Lord Nelson . . . . *(die)*?
    > Er, his last one, sir?

5   I . . . . *(buy)* this diamond ring from a man in the street. It's for my girlfriend.
    > Are they real diamonds?
    I hope so. If not, the man . . . . just . . . . *(cheat)* me out of £5.

6   How's your sister?
    > She . . . . *(go)* on a very strict diet to lose weight.
    And how is she getting on?
    > Fine. She . . . . *(disappear)* last week.

7   Mrs Smith is very upset. She thinks she . . . .
    (lose) her cat.
    > When . . . . she last . . . . *(see)* it?
    Four days ago.
    > Why doesn't she put an advertisement in
    the newspaper?
    Don't be silly. Her cat can't read.

"'A reward of £25 will be offered for the safe return of my cat.' Is that all she thinks of me!"

8   My dad . . . . never . . . . *(visit)*
    the dentist.
    > *My* dad will never go back to the dentist.
    Why? What happened?
    > The dentist . . . . *(take)* all his teeth out.
    What . . . . your dad . . . . *(say)*?
    > Never again! Never again!

9   Robert was fishing in a private lake. An old man came up to him and asked:
    > . . . . you . . . . *(catch)* anything?
    Yes. Three big fish since I . . . . *(start)* this morning.
    > My name is Lord Arton and I own this lake.
    Oh. My name is Robert and I'm a terrible liar!

It's been three years since I had a holiday.
Write some sentences about yourself using the pattern:
It's been ... since I ... (simple past) ... .

10 The Present Perfect Continuous

Complete the jokes with one of the following phrases:

ride a bike   *all its life*   *just won't go away*
in my pocket   *not yet*   *made it yet*
for 93 years   *lost your voice*

1   Who's been eating my porridge? said Baby Bear.
    > And who's been eating my porridge? said Daddy Bear.
    Don't get excited, said Mother Bear. I haven't . . . .

2   Paul, have you been fighting again? You've lost your two front teeth.
    > No, I haven't, Mum. They're . . . .

3   A salesman was speaking to a crowd. "Ladies and gentlemen. In this bottle I have the
    answer to old age. Drink this every day and you will never get old. You only have to look
    at me to see how good it is. I'm over 250 years old." An old woman went up to the
    salesman's young assistant and said, "Is it true? Is he really that age?"
    > I don't know, she replied. I've only been helping him . . . .

4   Your dog's been chasing a man on a bicycle.
    > Don't be silly. My dog can't . . . .

5   Have you been working here all your life?
    > . . . . !

6   A man was walking along a road kicking a tortoise.
    Why are you kicking this poor defenceless tortoise? asked a policeman.
    > Because it's been following me around all day and it . . . .

7   Did you wash the fish before cooking it?
    > No.
    Why not?
    > Well, what's the point in washing the fish when it has been swimming around in water
    . . . . ?

8   I've been singing since I was two years old.
    > No wonder you've . . . .

We often use the present perfect continuous to talk about actions repeated over a period of
time. *I have been smoking for five years.* Write some sentences about yourself using the
pattern: *I . . . . (present perfect continuous) . . . . for / since . . . . .*

11 The Past Perfect

Use *had* or *hadn't* to complete the following:

1 When her daughter arrived home from a party, Mrs Thompson asked her if she
. . . . thanked her hostess. "No," she said. "The girl in front of me thanked her and
the lady said 'Don't mention it' so I didn't."

2 Here's your coffee, madam – it's a special coffee all the way from Brazil.
> Oh, I was wondering where you . . . . gone.

3 A stressed managing director went to his doctor for help in getting to sleep. The workers
at his factory . . . . gone on strike. They wanted better pay and conditions. The
director . . . . tried sleeping pills but they . . . . worked. The doctor asked the
director to lie quite still in bed at night and to count sheep. The following day the
director returned to the doctor's surgery.
Well, said the doctor. Any success?
> I'm afraid not, he said. By the time I . . . . counted the thirty-first sheep they
. . . . all gone on strike for shorter hours and lower fences.

4 Kenneth is so stupid. He phoned his teacher at school yesterday to say he couldn't come
to school because he . . . . lost his voice!

5 A doctor . . . . just given a boy an injection in his arm. He was about to put a
bandage on his arm when the boy said,
Would you mind putting the bandage on my other arm, doctor?
> Why? I'm putting it over your vaccination so that the other boys will know not to
bang into it.
You don't know the boys in my school, doctor!

6 Mum! Mum! Dad's fallen over a cliff.
> Is he okay?
I don't know. He . . . .
stopped falling when I left.

7 A beggar stopped me the other day
and said he . . . . had a bite for days.
> What did you do?
I bit him!

8 It was my grandmother's birthday yesterday.
> Is she old?
Well, by the time we lit the last candle
on her birthday cake, the first one . . . . gone out!

9 Harry Smith was sent to Central Africa by his company. He sent a postcard to his wife
as soon as he arrived. Unfortunately it was delivered to another Mrs Smith whose
husband . . . . died the day before. The postcard read: ARRIVED SAFELY THIS
MORNING. THE HEAT IS TERRIBLE.

In spoken English *had* is often contracted to *'d* . Say the following by contracting had:
If only I had had your car!   What had she done?   He had lost his voice.
She had refused twice already!   They had asked him before.   Dad had done it.

**Look at the jokes again and change *had* to *'d* where possible. When is a contraction not
possible?**

12   The Past Perfect Continuous

Complete the jokes by putting these verbs in the gaps provided. Watch your spelling!

dig   follow   go   play   run   stand   walk   watch

1   Mrs Smith had been . . . . ing her doctor's advice for weeks but she wasn't feeling any better so she decided to visit the doctor again.
> The pills you gave me don't seem to be working. I still feel extremely tired.
Well, perhaps the problem is your diet. What have you been eating?
> Oh! exclaimed Mrs Smith. Am I supposed to eat as well?

2   Dad, was I walking when my little sister was born?
> Yes, you had been . . . . ing for six months.
Really? I must have been very tired then!

3   For weeks Gill had been . . . . . . ing past an expensive boutique on her way to work and each time she had stopped briefly to look in the window. One day she went in and said:
> Would you take that dress with red flowers out of the window, please?
Certainly, madam, replied the shop assistant.
> Thank you. It's been annoying me for weeks!

4   Peter had a very large garden and he had been . . . . ing it for about five hours when Mrs Burns came along.
Oh, hello, Peter. What are you growing?
The sweat was running down Peter's face.
He looked up and said, "Tired!"

Speech bubbles: Tired | What are you growing Peter?

5   A shopkeeper went over to the weighing machine in the corner of his shop to talk to a very fat boy who had been . . . . ing on the machine for about twenty minutes. The boy seemed to be having trouble reading the chart on the machine which showed how much people of different heights should weigh.
> So how much are you overweight?
I'm not overweight, said the boy indignantly, I'm just fifteen centimetres too short!

6   Two Native Americans were sitting on a hill looking across the countryside. They had been . . . . ing smoke signals from the next village all morning. One said to the other:
> What do you think?
I think somebody is writing a novel, the other replied.

7   There was a lot of snow. Paul and Robert were given a sledge by their father as a present. They had been . . . . . ing with it for about an hour when Paul suddenly rushed into the house with tears in his eyes. Robert soon followed.
Robert! shouted their father. I thought I told you to let Paul use the sledge half the time?
> But I did, dad. I had it going down and he had it going up!

8   Roger's face was very red because he had been . . . . ing up the street as fast as he could. As he came into the house his mother asked:
> Why are you running?
I was trying to stop a fight.
> Who was fighting?
Me and the big boy who has just moved into the house at the bottom of the street!

My face was hot and red because I'd been lying in the sun. Using your own experience or your imagination, try to complete this sentence in as many ways as you can:
My face was hot and red because I'd been ...-ing ... .

13 Will / going to – 1

Complete the jokes by putting *will ('ll)* or *(be) going to* in the gaps provided:

1   Darling, I want to see the world!
     > I . . . . give you an atlas for your next birthday, then.

2   I . . . . buy one of those small Japanese radios.
     > But how will you understand what they are saying?

3   Waiter, there's only one piece of meat on my plate.
     > Just wait a minute, sir, and I . . . . cut it in two.

4   A motorist ran over an old lady's cat and killed it.
     > I'm very sorry, said the motorist. I . . . . replace
     your cat, of course.
     Very well, but I hope you're good at catching mice.

5   What are you doing with that gun?
     > I . . . . shoot you.
     Why?
     > Because you look like me.
     I look like you?
     > Yes.
     Then shoot me!

6   How old are you now, Billy?
     > Seven.
     And what . . . . you . . . . do when you are big like your mother?
     > Stop eating chocolate!

7   Mummy, mummy! Where are you? cried a little boy at the beach.
     > You poor boy, said an old woman. Come with me and I . . . . get you an ice
     cream and then we . . . . go and look for your mummy.
     I know where your mother is, said a small girl. She's sitting ...
     > Be quiet, said the boy. I know as well, but this way I get a free ice-cream!

8   I have some good news for you and some bad news.
     > Tell me the bad news first, doctor.
     I . . . . amputate your legs.
     > And what is the good news?
     The man in the next bed wants to buy your shoes.

9   The British are planning to travel to the sun in a rocket next year, said a British scientist.
     > But, said an American scientist, as you get near the sun the heat will melt the rocket.
     We are not stupid, said the British scientist. We . . . . travel at night.

10   A circus was visiting a small town in France. The lion tamer walked into a bar and asked:
     > Do you serve Americans in here?
     Sure, said the barman.
     > Okay, I . . . . have a beer for myself, and two Americans for my lion outside!

Tell the class about some of the plans you have made recently. Try to use:
I'm definitely going to ...

14   Will / going to – 2

Complete the jokes by putting these words or phrases in the gaps provided:

die	*Emergency Exit*	*funeral*	*long*	*looks*
round	*sleep*	*sober*	*fly*	*wet*

1   Waiter, will my pizza be . . . . ?
    > No, I expect it will be round as usual.

2   Tomorrow my name will be up in lights in every cinema in the country.
    > How are you going to do that?
    Easy. I'm changing my name to . . . .

3   Two fish were swimming together in a river.
    > Look, said the first one. It's starting to rain.
    Quick. Let's swim under the bridge, said the second fish, or we'll get . . . .

4   Do you think I'll lose my . . . . as I get older?
    > If you're lucky!

5   The world will never come to an end.
    > Why?
    Because it is . . . . , stupid!

6   You're ugly.
    > And you're drunk.
    Yes, but in the morning
    I'll be . . . .

7   The television will never replace
    the newspaper.
    > Why?
    Because you can't swat a . . . .
    with a television.

8   I think I'm going to lose my job in the flower
    shop tomorrow.
    > What for?
    I sent flowers to a . . . . with the wrong card on them.
    > What did the card say?
    HOPE YOU'LL BE HAPPY IN YOUR NEW HOME.

9   I know what you're going to do tonight.
    > All right then. What am I going to do?
    You're going to . . . . , of course!

10 Doctor, help me. My heart is beating very quickly and I feel terrible. I think I'm going to
    . . . .
    > Nonsense. That's the last thing you'll do.

I don't think I'll ever get married. **Make some predictions about your future using the pattern:**
    I don't think I'll ever ...

15   Present used for future

The Present Simple and the Present Continuous can both be used to refer to events happening in the future. Underline the examples below which have future meaning. The first is done for you.

1   <u>We're sending</u> our son to a holiday camp next week.
    > Oh! Does he need a holiday?
    No, but we do!

2   I hear you're moving to London next week.
    > Yes, I have to because of my job.
    Are you working for the same people?
    > Yes – my wife and our six kids!

3   What are you giving your baby brother for
    Christmas this year?
    > I don't know.
    What did you give him last year?
    > Measles, I think.

4   A boy was up an apple tree stealing apples.
    A policeman came along and caught him.
    He looked up at the boy in the tree and said:
    > When are you coming down, young man?
    When you go away! replied the boy.

5   We're advertising for a new cashier in next week's Morning Post.
    > But you hired a new cashier last week!
    I know, but he isn't honest.
    > But you can't judge people by their appearance.
    I'm not. I'm judging him by his disappearance!

6   I begin work at the Swan Laundry on Monday.
    > That's wonderful! But tell me, how do you wash a swan?

7   My daughter gets married at three o'clock in St Mary's Church on Saturday.
    > How do you feel about it?
    Well, I'm losing a daughter but I am gaining a telephone!

8   Two farmers were talking about their plans.
    I'm growing a lot of beans next year. I think they will get a good price at the market.
    > Well, I'm growing mashed potatoes next year. People will buy them because they won't
    have to peel and cut the potatoes themselves.
    But how can you grow mashed potatoes?
    > Easy. You harvest the field with a steamroller!

9   A very boring speaker talked for two hours without stopping. When he finished he asked,
    Does anybody have a question?
    > Yes, said a voice from the back of the room. When are you leaving?

I'm flying to London on Friday. I'm staying the weekend with my sister. Then on Sunday I'm flying over to Paris for a meeting.
Write some sentences about your plans for this week and next. Use the present continuous.

16   The Future Continuous

Complete the jokes by putting these verbs in the gaps provided. Watch your spelling:

adopt	ask	entertain	need	drive
go	keep	leave	paint	use

1   That's the tenth game we've lost in a row and we haven't even scored a single goal,
shouted the angry manager of the football team, Hamstold United. The team captain who
had not scored a goal for twenty matches went up to the manager and said:
> Boss, I've got a great idea to improve the team.
The manager looked at the captain, then said, Wonderful! When will you be . . . . . ing?

2   Mrs Perkins was extremely rich and lived in a large country mansion. She phoned the
fishmonger to order some seafood.
> I will be . . . . ing some very important people this evening, she said in her
superior-sounding voice. So send me 25 oysters; not too small, not too large, not very old,
not tough and certainly not with any sand in them.
Certainly, madam, said the fishmonger. With or without pearls?

3   Patrick was a particularly mean person. Instead of buying things he usually tried to
borrow them. One Sunday he called at his next door neighbour's house and asked:
> Will you be . . . . ing your lawnmower this afternoon?
Yes! snapped his neighbour, determined not to give Patrick anything.
> Great! said Patrick. Then can I borrow your golf clubs? You won't be . . . . ing
them if you're cutting your grass!

4   Little Michael was pulling at his mother's dress in the kitchen to get her attention.
> What is it, Michael?
Will we be . . . . ing to see the monkeys as you promised?
> But why do you want to see the monkeys when your grandparents are here?

5   A famous female film star asked the artist, Pablo Cassels, to
paint her. Pablo was talking to his friend about it.
> Will you be . . . . ing her in the nude? asked the friend.
Oh no! said Pablo. I'll be . . . . ing my clothes on!

6   Waiter! There's a large mouse in my soup!
> Keep your voice down, sir. And don't wave
the mouse about or everybody else in the
restaurant will be . . . . ing for one!

I've got a large mouse!

7   Why do you want to learn French, Mr and Mrs Orr?
> Well, we'll be . . . . ing a little French baby
next month and we want to be able to understand
it when it begins to talk.

8   Derek Walton had driven coaches and taxis all his life but gave up because he was fed up
listening to critical passengers. However, he had no experience of any other kind of work.
He went to a job centre and after listening to his story, the officer said,
I can offer you a driving job in which you will never be troubled by back-seat drivers.
> And what will I be . . . . ing? asked Derek.
A hearse!

You'll recognise her when you see her. She'll be carrying a large blue bag.
How many ways can you think of to complete this sentence?
You'll recognise her when you see her. She'll be ...-ing ... .

17 Used to

Complete the jokes by using *used to* with one of the following verbs:

be	chase	dive	get	know	turn
saw	sit	study	take	be called	

1 And where did you learn to chop down trees, old man?
> In the Sahara desert in Africa.
But there aren't any trees in the Sahara, the young man replied.
> I know. But there . . . . !

2 Two magicians met at a party and started talking.
> What happened to the girl you . . . . in half?
Oh, she's now living in New York and San Francisco.

3 I wonder what happened to that silly blonde girl Peter
. . . .
> I dyed my hair!

4 In India when I was a young man in the army,
I . . . . wild elephants on horses.
> Really? I never knew that elephants could ride horses.

5 I worked in a circus when I was in my twenties.
> What did you do?
I . . . . into a bucket of water from a height
of six metres. Then I broke my neck.
> What happened? Did you miss the bucket?
No. Some idiot had emptied the water out.

6 I learned to swim at an early age. When I was three my parents . . . .
me out to sea in a little boat and throw me into the water.
> Wasn't that a difficult way to learn to swim?
Well, the swimming was easy – it was getting out of the sack that was the difficult bit.

7 I . . . . into a werewolf once a month but I'm all right nowoooowoowooo!

8 Our cat . . . . Tom. Now it's called Isabelle.
> Why did you change its name?
It had five kittens last week.

9 David, you . . . . very good marks in your class tests. I just don't
understand why you're now at the bottom of the class.
> It's the teacher's fault.
What do you mean?
> I . . . . next to the boy who is always top of the class but the teacher
moved me to another seat and now I can't copy from him!

10 I . . . . French, German and Algebra at school.
> Funny! I've never heard anybody speak Algebra.

Think of someone in your family who is over 60 years old. What was life like when they were young? You can start your sentences in the following ways:

Things were different then.   *People used to ...*   *People never used to ...*
This town was different then.   *There used to be ...*   *There never used to be ...*
Schools were different then.   *Cars were different in those days.*

18   Have / have got

Complete the jokes by putting *has (or 's)* / *have(or 've)* / *hasn't* or *haven't* in the gaps provided:

1   Is this a second-hand shop?
> Yes.
Good! . . . . you got a second hand for my watch?

2   I . . . . got a terrible problem. I . . . . got a flat in London and a house in Paris.
I . . . . got four cars and one of them is a Rolls-Royce. I . . . . got a boat and a
private plane.
> So what's the problem?
I . . . . got any money to pay for them.

3   I . . . . got some good news for you, Mrs Smith.
> It's Miss Smith, doctor.
Well, Miss Smith. I . . . . got some bad news for you.

4   What . . . . got a neck but . . . . got a head?
> I don't know.
A bottle.

5   Excuse me, ... you got a cigarette?
> Yes. I . . . . got lots of them.

6   What . . . . got four legs and flies?
> I don't know.
A dead cat.

7   What two words . . . . got
thousands of letters in them?
> I don't know.
Post Office.

8   Two men are playing at cards.
> I win. I . . . . got four aces.
I'm afraid I win.
> That's impossible. What . . . . you got?
Two nines and a loaded gun.
> OK. You win!

9   Mum, there's a salesman at the door with a moustache.
> Tell him your father . . . . already got one.

10   My grandmother is 83 and she . . . . got one grey hair on her head.
> That's amazing!
No, it's not. She's bald!

---

1. **Think of all your friends. What kind of cars have they got?**
    John's got a Saab.   I've got an old Nissan.
2. **Think of people you know who aren't very well. What's the matter with them?**
    My sister's got a cold.   Nigel's got a bad back.
3. **Think of your computer. How much memory has it got? What software have you got?**
    It's got 20 megabytes of RAM. I've got Wordperfect.

Go round the class, Student 1 starts: I've got (something beginning with A). Then student 2:
*I've got (the word Student 1 used) and (a word beginning with B). Student 3: I've got (the
two things already mentioned) and (a word beginning with C). And so on.*

19   The Imperative

Complete the jokes with one of the following:

You're a taxi	*teeth*	*4 to 6 years*	*bath*	*Which one*
You love me	*six cows*	*Jack, Queen, King*	*sore head*	*yes, no, yes, no*

1   Billy is on his new bicycle.
> Look, mum. No hands.
A minute later he shouts,
> Look, mum. No feet.
Five minutes later he shouts,
> Look, mum. No . . . . !

2   Oh Harry, say you love me! Say you love me!
> Okay. . . . . !

3   John, walk to the back of the bus and tell me if
the indicators are working.
John walks to the back of the bus and shouts:
> . . . . !

4   Graham. Spell cattle.
> C-A-T-T-T-L-E
Leave out one of the Ts, Graham.
> . . . . ?

5   Waiter, call me a taxi, please.
> Okay, sir. . . . .

6   What is frozen tea?
> Iced tea.
And what is frozen beer?
> Iced beer.
And what is frozen ink?
> Iced ink.
Well, have a . . . . , then!

7   Name ten things with milk in them.
> Cheese, yoghurt, chocolate, my dad's tea and ... er ... and . . . .

8   Look at that notice. It says:
TAKE ASPIRIN FOR A HEADACHE.
> What a stupid advertisement!
Why?
> Well, who wants a . . . . ?

9   Paul, count up to ten in English for me.
> Yes, miss. One, two, three, four, five, six, seven, eight, nine, ten.
Very good. Now continue.
> Yes, miss. . . . . !

10 How old is our teacher?
> I don't know but I know how to find out.
How?
> Look inside his shirt.
But how does that tell us his age?
> Well, in my shirt it says . . . .

What are the most common commands a) in the army b) in your class c) in your home?

Section Two
Modal Verbs

The English Modals

Here is a list of the English modals:

can / could	may / might	will / would	shall / should
must	ought to		

Modals are not full verbs like *eat* or *sleep*. They allow us to express an idea which is not a fact – very often our attitude to an event. For example:

possibility   John can play the violin.
impossibility   Sorry, I can't make your party on Saturday. I'm in France.
a condition   I would if I could.
advice   You ought to try Nurofen. It's far better than ordinary aspirin.
deduction   Ah, you must be John. I recognised your car.

Small differences in meaning

Sometimes there is very little difference in meaning between a modal use and a non-modal use:

I *speak* German.   *I'm going to* get the 7 o'clock flight.
I *can speak* German.   *I'll get* the 7 o'clock flight.

Sometimes two modals can seem similar in meaning:

I *may* be late.   You *must* come.
I *might* be late.   You *ought* to come.

Serious differences in meaning

The differences between *We must be here by 9; We'll have to be here by 9; We have to be here by 9* are small, but the following difference is serious:

We *mustn't* arrive by 7.
We *don't have to* arrive by 7.

Notice also the relationship between the following pairs:

1.   You *must* take the tablets before eating.
      You *mustn't* take them before going to bed.

2.   That *must* be her husband. He's getting out of her car.
      That *can't* be her husband. He's old enough to be her father.

20 Can / could – ability

Complete the jokes by putting *can, can't, could,* or *couldn't* in the gaps provided:

1 My father . . . . lift a pig with one hand. . . . . your dad do that?
   > I'm not sure. Where do you get a pig with one hand?

2 What do you call a man with no ears?
   > Anything you like because he . . . . hear you.

3 Waiter, I . . . . eat this soup.
   > I'm sorry, sir. I'll get the manager.
   (Manager arrives.)
   I'm afraid I . . . . eat this soup.
   > I'm sorry, sir. I'll call the cook.
   (Cook arrives.)
   I'm sorry, but I . . . . eat this soup.
   > Why not, sir?
   Because I don't have a spoon!

I don't have a spoon . . !

4 Why . . . . a car play football?
   > I don't know.
   Because it only has one boot.

5 Angela, since I met you I . . . . eat
   and I . . . . drink.
   > Oh Bruce! Is it because you love me so much?
   No. It's because I haven't got any money left.

6 What . . . . you make that you . . . . see?
   > I don't know.
   A noise.

7 Why are you hitting your dog with a chair?
   > Because I . . . . lift the table!

8 I'd like three large fish and I want you to throw them to me, said a fisherman.
   > But why? said the shopkeeper.
   So that I . . . . tell my wife that I caught three fish.

9 *(In a library)* Please be quiet. The other people in here . . . . read.
   > Oh, what a pity. I . . . . read when I was six.

10 Why did you buy that hat?
    > Because I . . . . get it for nothing!

I'd like to be able to sing. I'd love to be able to play the piano. I'd love to be able to fly a plane.
Write down some of the things you can't do but want to do. Use the pattern: *I'd like / love to be able to … .*

21   Can / could – requests

Complete the jokes by putting the words in brackets in the correct order:

1   Can I have a pair of crocodile shoes, please?
     > Sure. *(size take crocodile what your does)*
     . . . . ?

2   A woman ran into a shop and said,
     > Do you have a mousetrap, please?
     Certainly, madam.
     > And could you be quick? I have a bus to catch.
     I'm sorry, madam. *(that make we traps don't big)*
     . . . .

3   Dad, can I leave the table?
     > Well, *(it you with certainly you take can't)*
     . . . .

4   Do you want to come to the cinema with me?
     > Not with you!
     Well, could you give me 10p to phone a friend?
     > Here's 20 pence. *(all them phone of)* . . . .

5   Hello, Mrs Brown. Can James come out to play?
     > I'm afraid not. He's sick and he's in bed.
     Oh ... *(out his can bike play to come)* . . . . ?

6   Mum, now that I'm sixteen, can I wear lipstick and put on make-up? Can I use nail
     varnish and wear short skirts?
     > *(can't no you John)* . . . .

7   Tommy, your father says you broke the kitchen window with your football. Is this true?
     > Yes, mum, but it was an accident.
     Could you tell me what your father said to you?
     > Can I leave out the swear words?
     Of course.
     > Well then, *(say didn't he anything)* . . . .

8   Tailor, could you make me a suit in one week?
     > I'm afraid not. It takes six weeks to make a suit.
     Six weeks! But God made the world in one week!
     > I know. *(at in state the is look but the world)* . . . .

9   An old lady was at the side of the road. A boy came along.
     > Young man, the old lady said. Can you see me across the road?
     I don't know, said the boy. *(go a have I'll and look)* . . . .

10   Waiter, can you get me some undercooked potatoes, some cold beans and a cold fried egg
     covered in fat?
     > I'm sorry, sir, but we couldn't give you anything like that.
     Why not? *(me gave what yesterday that's you)* . . . .

Can you help me? What other words and phrases can replace *can* in this sentence to make a
request? Complete the pattern in as many ways as you can.
Can I borrow your pencil sharpener for a second? Using this pattern, write down some of the
common requests that you make in class / at home / at work / on the beach.

22 Must / have to

Complete the jokes below with one of the following phrases:

> on the toilet door   stop it
> spend it for you   look at it
> go back tomorrow   fight for them
> stop her   have a door
> wake up until seven o'clock the headmaster

1 Does your watch tell the time?
> No, you have to . . . .

2 Did you know that every four seconds a woman gives birth to a child?
> That's terrible. We must find this woman and . . . .

3 I'm not going to school today. The teachers don't like me. The children hate me and the caretaker is rude to me.
> But you have to go to school for two very good reasons.
What are they?
> You're forty years old and you're

. . . .

4 A young boy arrived home with a black eye.
> Who gave you the black eye? shouted his mother.
They don't give you one of these, mother. You have to . . . .

5 I'm having a problem breathing, doctor.
> Well, I must give you something to

. . . .

"You have to go to school!"

6 I have a problem. I have to go to the toilet at six o'clock in the morning.
> Why is that a problem?
I don't . . . .

7 Mrs Robinson was very worried about her weight because she wanted to look good for her holiday at the seaside. On a bus one day she said to the woman sitting next to her:
> I must get rid of twenty pounds but I don't know how to do it.
That's easy, give it to me and I'll . . . .

8 You have to whistle loudly in our house.
> Why is that?
Because there's no lock . . . . !

9 Did you enjoy your first day at school, son?
> What! Do you mean I have to . . . . ?

10 I had to get up early this morning to open the door in my pyjamas.
> That's a strange place to . . . .

We often use *had to* to make excuses. Complete this conversation with good excuses:

Why didn't you come to the party last night?
Sorry, but I had to ... .

23   Mustn't / don't have to

Complete the jokes with *mustn't* or *don't have to*:

1   You . . . . pull the cat's tail.
    > I'm only holding it. It's the cat that's pulling.

2   Dad, I can help you to save some money.
    > Really! How can you do that?
    Do you remember saying you'd give me £10 for passing my exams?
    > Yes.
    Well, you . . . . pay me now.

3   Well, Stevens, do you really want to work in this office?
    > Yes, sir!
    First, you have to be clean to work here. Did you
    wipe your feet on the mat?
    > Yes, sir.
    Second, Stevens. If you want to work here,
    you . . . . tell lies.
    > What do you mean, sir?
    There is no mat at the door!

4   Oh darling! You . . . . leave me!
    > But I can't leave you.
    Is that because you love me so much, darling?
    > No, it's because you're standing on my foot!

"You mustn't leave me! I couldn't stand it!"

5   It's 40°C out there. We'll need an air-conditioned
    coach to take the team to the stadium.
    > We . . . . spend extra money on an air-conditioned coach. An ordinary
    coach will be fine.
    But won't it be too hot for the players?
    > Don't worry. We'll have thirty fans travelling with us!

6   A young boy fell off his bicycle and hurt his head. He was in an ambulance which was
    taking him to hospital. He was a little confused.
    > Tell me your name, said the nurse.
    Why? asked the boy.
    > So that we can tell your parents.
    Oh, you . . . . do that. They already know my name!

7   Christopher, is there any difference between lightning and electricity? asked the Physics
    teacher.
    > Er ... I think so, sir.
    And what is that difference?
    > You . . . . pay for lightning, sir.

8   Let's go shopping.
    > That's a good idea but I . . . . forget to visit the optician. I think I need glasses.
    What makes you think that?
    > Well, yesterday I turned the knobs on the oven and an orchestra started playing!

You don't have to wear a uniform. **Make up some similar sentences using the pattern:**
At work / At school / On holiday / In summer / Among friends – you don't have to ...

24 Must / can't

Complete the jokes using *must* or *can't*:

1   You . . . . have a really clean kitchen in this restaurant.
    > We like to think so, sir. But how can you tell?
    Well, everything I've eaten tastes like soap.

2   Excuse me. Are there any policemen around here?
    > You . . . . be joking! You can never find a policeman when you need one.
    Great! Now give me all your money or I'll shoot you.

3   A tourist from Central Asia travelled to the
    seaside for the first time. He saw a man filling
    bottles with sea water.
    > How much are they? he asked.
    Thirty roubles, replied the man.
    The tourist bought two bottles and returned
    five hours later when the tide was out.
    > Gosh! he said to the man. You . . . .
    have made a fortune!

4   The last person in this room was an inventor.
    He invented explosives.
    > So these marks on the ceiling . . . . be
    explosives?
    No, that's the inventor.

5   I saw ten men standing under one umbrella and
    none of them got wet.
    > It . . . . have been a very big umbrella.
    No. It wasn't raining.

6   This . . . . be my shirt. The collar is so tight I can hardly breathe.
    > Don't be silly. You've put your head through a button-hole.

7   Waiter, there's a fly in my soup.
    > The spider . . . . have missed it, sir.

8   Mummy, why do you have so many grey hairs?
    > Probably because you're such a naughty child and I worry about you a lot.
    You can talk! Looking at grandmother, you . . . . have been a very good child either.

9   Do you think our son got his intelligence from me?
    > He . . . . have done. I've still got mine.

10 A drunk man was standing next to a street lamp post, trying to put his key into it. A
    woman walked up to him and said sarcastically, "I don't think there's anybody at home."
    The man slowly lifted his head and with difficulty he said, "There . . . . be
    somebody in because there's a light on upstairs."

You must be joking! You can't be serious!
Work in pairs. Student A says something which will make Student B use one of the above
responses. Take turns. For example:
Student A: *The Prime Minister has just resigned.*
Student B: *You must be joking!*

25 Should / shouldn't

Complete the jokes by putting *should* or *shouldn't* in the gaps provided:

1   You . . . . pay your taxes with a smile.
    > I tried that but they wanted cash.

2   Someone has been eating the pie I cooked yesterday. . . . . I call the police?
    > I think an ambulance might be a better idea!

3   Doctor, how can I live to be a hundred?
    > You . . . . smoke or drink alcohol. You . . . . only eat bread and drink
    milk and you . . . . live alone in the countryside.
    And will I live to be a hundred?
    > I don't know, but it'll certainly seem like it.

4   I'm in love with two girls. One is very beautiful but has no money, the other is ugly and
    has lots of money. Who . . . . I marry?
    > Well, I'm sure that you must really love the beautiful one, so I think you . . . .
    marry her.
    OK, thank you very much for your advice.
    > Don't mention it. By the way, I wonder if you could give me the name and telephone
    number of the other girl?

5   Why do you think I . . . . sell you this television for half price?
    > Because I only have one eye!

6   Doctor, every time I try to take this young man's
    pulse it gets much faster. . . . . I give him
    a sedative?
    The doctor looked at the pretty young
    nurse and replied:
    > No, but the next time you take the
    patient's temperature, put a blindfold
    on him first!

7   A priest saw two little boys fighting outside the church.
    You . . . . fight, he said to the bigger boy. Remember, you . . . . love your
    enemy.
    > But he's not my enemy, said the boy. He's my brother.

8   Doctor, I know I . . . . steal cars but I can't stop myself. Can you help me?
    > Take these pills. They should do the trick.
    But what if they don't work?
    > Then get me a Ferrari!

9   I have a terrible headache and my doctor can't cure it.
    > You . . . . change to my doctor. You'll never live to regret it.

You shouldn't smoke. **Give your advice on healthy living by writing down some sentences
using *should* or *shouldn't*.**
Should you or shouldn't you? – *sleep ten hours a night, cut out sugar and salt from your diet,
cut out all alcohol consumption, take regular exercise, get out into the fresh air, sleep with a
window open, get angry, stay up late watching films on TV, avoid all forms of stress, take
regular holidays, eat meat, become a vegetarian, eat lots of fruit and vegetables.*

26 Should have / shouldn't have

Complete the jokes by putting *should* or *shouldn't* in the gaps provided:

1   I've got some good news and some bad news for you. Which would you like first?
> Give me the good news, doctor.
OK. The good news is you've got six weeks to live.
> If that's the good news, what's the bad news?
I . . . . have told you five weeks ago!

2   I don't think my parents . . . . have had children. I don't think they really know much about bringing them up.
> Why do you say that?
Well, they always put me to bed when I'm wide awake and they wake me up when I'm fast asleep.

3   Wilson, you . . . . have been in class at nine o'clock this morning.
> Why, sir? Did I miss something exciting?

4   I went swimming after lunch and got cramp.
> Well, you . . . . have been swimming on a full stomach.
But I wasn't! I was swimming on my back!

5   So, your cat's just had ten kittens, Mrs Jackson.
> Yes, I don't know how she managed it. I just can't understand it. Tabby has never been out of the house.
The vet saw a large male cat in the corner of the room and said:
I don't think you . . . . have left Tabby alone with that cat over there.
> Oh don't be silly, said Mrs Jackson. That's Tabby's brother.

6   Can I speak to Mr Stevens, please?
> I'm afraid not. He's not in the office. You could try again in an hour or so.
But he . . . . have left his office at this time in the morning. Where is he?
> Oh. He's out having lunch with his wife at the Luxor Hotel.
Well, when he gets back, tell him his secretary called!

7   Why are you crying?
> I washed my canary in soap powder and it died.
That's stupid. You . . . . have used soap powder. You . . . . have washed it gently with warm water.
> But it wasn't the soap powder that killed it. It was the spin drier!

8   Billy's father returned from watching his local football team. They had lost the match and he was very unhappy with one of his team's players.
> What a terrible player he is! He . . . . never have been playing today.
Seven-year-old Billy thought for a moment, then said:
> Maybe it was his ball, Dad.

9   A visitor was walking round the gardens of a monastery on a very hot and sunny day. He was admiring the lovely flowers and plants in the garden and said,
How wonderful the works of God are!
The old monk working in the garden lifted his head and said:
> Yes, but you . . . . have seen the garden when He had it to Himself!

In spoken English *have* is often contracted to *'ve*. Look at the jokes again and change *have* to *'ve* where possible. Practise saying the sentences with the contracted form.

Section Three
Conditionals

Three common patterns

When teaching or learning English, it is common to talk about the First, Second, and Third Conditionals:

1. I'll scratch your back, if you scratch mine.

2. If we arrived early, we'd get the best seats.

3. If you'd saved the file, you wouldn't have lost all your work when your computer crashed.

Other patterns

The reason we talk about those three is because they are the most common patterns, but there are many more patterns in sentences with *if*:

1. It is common to use modals in conditionals:

   If only you'd asked me, I would have lent you the money!
   If you must smoke, do it outside, please.
   If you want my opinion, I'd sell the car and buy something more reliable.

2. Some conditionals use the present simple in both parts:

   If the order comes in today, we get a bonus.
   If it rains, the water comes in through the roof.

3. You use the past simple in both parts to talk about something that happened regularly in the past.

   If it was sunny, we went down to the beach with a picnic.
   If it rained we stayed indoors and played Monopoly or cards.

A good rule

A good 'rule' for students is to avoid using *would* in the *if-clause*. This is almost always true.

27   The First Conditional

Complete the jokes by putting the words (in brackets) in the right order:

1   A famous film director was shouting at a group of actors. The company doctor said,
> If (all shout time you the) ...., you'll get an ulcer.
The director looked at the doctor and replied:
> I don't get ulcers, I give them.

2   Anne, why do doctors wear masks when they operate?
> So that nobody will recognise them if (wrong goes anything) ....!

3   I want to live to a very old age.
> That's easy. If (months every apple for eat day an you 1200) ....
..........................., you'll live to be 100 years old.

4   The diamond necklace looks wonderful on you, madam.
> Yes, it does, doesn't it? But if (it like husband my doesn't) ....,
will you refuse to take it back?

5   On the ferry to France, you must all be very careful, said the headmaster. If a student falls
into the sea, what will you do?
> Shout "Boy overboard", sir.
And what will you do if (into sea a falls teacher the)
.........................?
There was a moment of silence, then a voice said:
> It would depend which one, sir!

6   Darling, what do you do with all the money I give you?
> Well, dear. If (in mirror you the of front stand)
.....................,
you'll soon see where it goes!

7   Do you think I have a gift for playing the piano?
> No, but (one give you I'll) ....,
if you stop playing!

8   What shall we do tonight?
> Let's toss a coin to decide.
Okay.
> If it's heads, we'll watch television and if it's tails we'll play football.
But if (lands it edge on its) ...., we'll do our homework!

9   Doctor, I feel like a pack of cards.
> If (down sit you) ...., I'll deal with you in a minute.

10 Jones, if (£5.50 you £20.45 and give I) ...., what will you have?
> A smile on my face, sir!

If I pass my exams, I'll apply for a place at university. Write similar sentences about your
future, using the pattern: *If I ... , I'll / won't ...* . For example:
   If I get home early tonight, ...
   If I get a wage rise this year, ...
   If I decide to go abroad on holiday this year, ...
   If I don't get home on time, ...

28   The Second Conditional

Complete the jokes by putting *would* or *wouldn't* in the gaps provided:

1   If you had 20 apples in your right hand and 30 in your left, what . . . . you have?
     > Sore arms.

2   A doctor asked three men what they . . . . do if he told them they only had one month left to live.
     > I . . . . stop work, live quietly, and prepare to die, replied the first man.
     > I . . . . take all my money out of the bank and spend it, said the second man.
     > I . . . . get a second opinion, said the third man.

3   Spell blind bird.
     > b-l-i-n-d-b-i-r-d
     Wrong. It's b-l-n-d b-r-d because if it had two i's, it . . . . be blind!

4   What . . . . you do if you were in my shoes?
     > Polish them.

5   What . . . . happen if I cut off your left ear?
     > I . . . . be able to hear.
     And what . . . . happen if I cut off your right ear?
     > I . . . . be able to see.
     Why?
     > Because my glasses would have fallen off!

6   Pauline, what is a "cannibal"?
     > I don't know, sir.
     Well, if you ate your mother and father,
     what . . . . you be?
     > An orphan, sir?

7   Don't you think I sing with feeling?
     > No. If you had any feeling, you . . . . sing.

8   A young boy came home with a pain in his stomach.
     Sit down, said his mother. Your stomach's hurting because it's empty. It'll be all right when you've got something in it.
     An hour later the boy's father came home from work, complaining of a headache.
     > That's because it's empty, said the son. You . . . . be all right if you had something in it!

9   Tell me straight, doctor. Is it serious?
     > Well, I . . . . start watching any new television serials if I were you.

10   If you had 25 pence and you asked your grandmother for 30 pence and your grandfather for 40 pence, how much . . . . you have?
     > 25 pence, sir.
     You don't know your arithmetic, do you?
     > And you don't know my grandparents, sir!

If I met the Queen, I'd ask her what she does in the evenings.
Think of famous people you'd like to meet and write similar sentences with the pattern:
     If I met... , I'd ask ... .
     If I met the American President / a top tennis player / Leonardo di Caprio / the Pope ...

29   The Third Conditional

Complete the jokes by putting the correct form of these verbs into the gaps provided:

be	take	steal	win
give	buy	fail	stay

1   Men, I'm sorry to tell you that Corporal Wright was killed by a tiger on a jungle path last night because he didn't think quickly enough. Private Smith, if you had . . . . in the Corporal's shoes, what steps would you have taken?
> Great big ones, sir!

2   A man paid £1000 for a dog that could talk. He took it to a friend and said:
> Look at this. I have a dog that talks.
Don't be stupid, his friend said. I'll bet you £30 it can't talk.
The dog said nothing and the man had to pay his friend £30. He was furious.
> Why didn't you say something, you stupid animal? If you had said something, I would have . . . . £30.
Not so stupid, said the dog. Just think of the money you'll win next time.

3   When we arrived at the airport this morning, there was a man running up and down shouting, "Take a bus, take a train but don't take a plane. It's wrong to fly. If God had meant people to fly, he would have . . . . them wings."
> Who was the man?
Our pilot!

4   What did you do today, Andrew?
> I went swimming in the river.
But where did you leave your clothes?
> On the river bank.
But what would you have done if somebody had . . . . your clothes?
Andrew thought for a moment and said:
> Waited until it was dark before trying to get home.

5   Harry says that if I had . . . . you some ice-cream at the cinema last night, you would have let me kiss you.
> Nonsense.
Well, what would I have to give you to get a kiss?
> An anaesthetic!

6   A famous surgeon had just returned from a hunting trip in Africa. When he came into work, a patient asked him how he had got on.
> Oh, it was very disappointing, the surgeon replied. I didn't kill a thing. I would have been better off if I had . . . . here in the hospital.

7   If it had taken ten men ten days to build a wall, how long would five men have . . . . ?
> No time at all, sir.
What do you mean?
> Well, the ten men have already built the wall!

8   Flight BA 324 had just arrived at Heathrow Airport after an emergency landing. During the flight three of the four engines had had to be shut down because of problems. A passenger went up to the pilot as he was leaving the plane.
> What would have happened if the last engine had . . . . ?
The pilot looked at the man and smiled sardonically:
> We would all have had to get out and push!

What would you have done if you had been on the Titanic / been held hostage / been on a plane which was hijacked / lost all your money and credit cards on holiday abroad?

30 Wish / if only

Complete the jokes by putting these words or phrases in the gaps provided:

> half an hour ago   the name   that much money   tickets   piano practice
> will power   will   your own coffee   history   car keys

1   I wish I had enough money to buy twenty elephants
     > But what do you want 20 elephants for?
     I don't. I just wish I had . . . . !

2   Mr and Mrs Smith have just arrived at the airport to catch a plane to London.
     > I wish I had brought the piano with me, said Mr Smith.
     What on earth for? said his wife.
     > Because I've left our . . . . on it!

3   Mary was meeting her friend, Sheila, who was
     an incredibly mean person.
     > How are things with you?
     I'm short of cash at the moment. If only I had
     ten pence for every man who asked me to
     marry him.
     > Yes, then you just might be able to pay for
     . . . . !

4   I'd like 100 grams of acetysalicylic acid in tablet form, please.
     > You mean, said the chemist, you'd like some aspirins, sir?
     That's right. I can never remember . . . . !

5   If only I had been born two thousand years ago.
     > Why, son?
     Because there wouldn't be so much . . . . to learn.

6   I wish you would stop playing that trumpet. I think I'm going mad!
     > I stopped playing . . . . , dad!

7   Mrs Arnott is standing on a deserted beach with her two children. She is angry.
     > You children are always causing problems. If only you could remember where you
     buried dad in the sand!
     Why is that a problem, mum?
     > Because the . . . . are in his pocket and we can't get home without them.

8   Mrs Smith's husband died three weeks ago. A kindly neighbour is visiting her.
     > And how are you coping now, Margaret?
     Fine, said Mrs Smith, but my husband's . . . . has caused so many problems
     that I now wish he hadn't died in the first place!

9   A poor starving man walked up to a very rich, fat lady and said:
     > I haven't had a single meal all week.
     If only I had your . . . . , replied the lady as she walked away.

10   Do you like your new flat?
     > Yes, but I wish my neighbours wouldn't bang on the wall at two o'clock in the morning.
     That's awful. Does it keep you awake?
     > No, but it certainly interferes with my . . . . !

I wish I had gone to university. **What regrets do you have in your life? Write down some
sentences about yourself using the pattern:** *I wish + (I had ... or I hadn't ...).*

31   Unless / if not

Complete these jokes using the following expressions:

my daughter's name	*sew the hole in my shirt*	*you can't sleep in class*
I'm drowning	*in the window*	*lose all my pigeons*
kill yourself	*your daughter*	*don't bite any*

1   Doctor, will I be all right in Africa?
    > You'll be fine unless you get a disease from biting insects.
    But doctor, how can I avoid diseases from biting insects?
    > Simple! . . . . !

2   If you don't come out of the water immediately, I will have to arrest you. Swimming is
    not allowed. This is private property. Didn't you see the sign?
    > Yes, officer, I saw the sign.
    Well, why are you swimming in a private lake?
    > I'm not swimming, officer. . . . . !

3   I'm getting married next Friday, sir. Can I have the day off?
    > Married! No woman would marry you unless she was mad! Who are you marrying?
    . . . . !

4   It was a very hot afternoon and David was having trouble keeping his eyes open.
    > David, wake up. . . . . , shouted the teacher.
    David lifted his head from his desk and said:
    > Well, sir, if you didn't talk so loudly, I'm sure I would be able to!

5   If my brothers don't leave home soon, I'll have to
    look for somewhere else to stay. One has six cats;
    another has four dogs; and my youngest brother has
    three pigs!
    > So, what's the problem?
    We all live in one room and the smell is terrible.
    > Why don't you open the window?
    What! And . . . . !

6   Young lady: If I don't kiss you, will you
                  . . . . ?
    Young man: That's what I usually do.

"Why don't you open the window?"

7   I'd like a return ticket to Cairo, please.
    > There you are. That's £480.
    Oh, I'd also like a ticket for Oninda.
    > Is that in Nigeria? I can't issue a ticket if I
    don't know where it is!
    I'm sorry. Oninda is . . . .

8   I'm afraid that the cut on your arm won't stop bleeding unless I put some stitches in it.
    > Go ahead, doctor.
    (After some time) There you are. Eighteen stitches.
    > Thanks, doctor. Can I ask one more thing?
    Certainly. What is it?
    > Could you . . . . while you've got your needle and thread out?

9   I'd like to try on that dress . . . . if I may.
    > I'm sorry, madam. You can't – not unless you use the fitting room like everyone else!

Underline all the uses of *unless* and *if ... not*. Is it possible to change one to the other? In all
the examples?

Section Four

Passives

What is the passive?

A passive structure uses part of the verb *(be)* plus the past participle form of the verb:

> A dog bit Peter.
> Peter was bitten by a dog.

In one sense they have the same meaning. Each contains the same three ideas of *Peter + dog + bite*. The second sentence, however, is 'not just another way' to say the first one.

Why use the passive and not the active?

The question we must ask is *what is the sentence about?* In the two sentences above, the first is about *a dog* (that is why it is mentioned first) and the second sentence is about *Peter*. The structure – active or passive – depends on how the sentence starts. Sometimes the passive is the more natural choice. Think of the situations where you would read the following and you will see why the passive is the obvious choice:

1. Children must be carried.
2. Outdoor shoes must not be worn in the gym.
3. These gates will be locked at 8pm daily.
4. Hard hats must be worn at all times.

No. 1 is a sign in the London Underground at the top and bottom of escalators. It has more impact than *If you have a child with you, please carry him or her.*

No. 2 is a sign in a school outside the gymnasium. It is more direct than *You mustn't wear your outdoor shoes in the gym.*

No. 3 is a sign on the gates of a park warning people to be out of the park before the gates are locked. Warning signs are always as short as possible.

No. 4 is a common sign on building sites. Again, it is an important safety sign and needs to be as short as possible. *You must wear a hard hat at all times* does not have the impact or authority of the passive.

32 Passives – present and past

Complete the jokes by putting the verb in brackets in the correct present passive *(is done)* or past passive *(was done)* form. Be careful, some are questions.

1 Nice to meet you, Mr Green. And how is your family?
> Terrible. My wife . . . . *(hit)* by a car yesterday. My son . . . .
(attack) at a football match. My daughter . . . . *(rob)* at a bus stop.
That's awful. What exactly do you do?
> I'm a fortune-teller.

2 Waiter, there's a dead fly in my soup.
> Yes. I'm afraid it . . . . *(kill)* by the heat, sir.

3 An old lady was talking to a young boy in the park.
And do you go to school?
> No, said the boy. I . . . .
(send).

4 We're famous for snails in this
restaurant, sir.
> I know. I . . . .
(serve) by one now.

5 What did your father say when you
. . . . *(take)*
to prison?
> Hello, son.

6 What kind of ants
. . . .
(find) in houses?
> I don't know.
OccupANTS!

7 What happened when the wheel . . . . *(invent)?*
> I don't know.
It caused a revolution!

8 A teacher asked her class to write an essay about a football match. A minute later all the
students were writing except one boy. The teacher looked at his paper. It said,
> The game . . . . *(stop)* in the first minute by rain.

9 Why . . . . the tennis player . . . . *(give)* a cigarette lighter at the end of
the competition?
> I don't know.
Because he had lost all his matches!

10 Mum, do all fairy tales begin with "Once upon a time"?
> No, darling. Some start with, "Sorry I'm so late, darling, I . . . .
(detain) at the office.

---

1. Write some sentences using the simple past passive to talk about your own life. For
example:
    I was injured in a car accident in 1991.
Try to use the following verbs: *injured, hurt, invited to, congratulated, introduced to, helped.*

2. Make up sentences about the following disasters:
Titanic – drowned / saved; Chernobyl – killed; Vesuvius – covered / killed.

33 Passives – perfect

Complete the jokes by putting the verbs given in the correct perfect passive form *(have / had been done)*. If the verb phrase contains *just, already, ever* or *never*, make sure you put it in the correct place.

1   Why are you putting a bandage on your pay cheque?
    > Because my salary . . . . . . just . . . . *(cut)*.

2   . . . . your eyes ever . . . . *(check)*?
    > As far as I know they've always been plain blue.

3   A man went to a hospital for a new brain. He was given a choice between two brains
    – an engineer's for £20,000 or a politician's for £500,000.
    Does that mean the politician's brain is much better?
    > Not exactly, said the doctor. The politician's brain . . . . . . never . . . . *(use)*.

4   Sadly, the only son of the director of a large company . . . . *(kill)* in a car
    accident. An ambitious employee approached the boy's father:
    I was wondering, sir, if it would be possible for me to take your son's place?
    > Certainly, replied the director. I'll see if the undertaker can arrange it.

5   I . . . . *(ask)* to get married hundreds of times.
    > Oh! Who by?
    My parents.

6   Why are you crying, Robert?
    > Well, Grandad, I want to play Cowboys and
    Indians and dad won't play with me.
    I'll play with you, then.
    > That's no good, Grandad, because you
    . . . . . . already . . . . *(scalp)*!

"Scalped!"

7   A man was visiting a friend in hospital.
    You . . . . *(miss)* by
    everybody at the factory.
    > That's nice.
    Yes. Yesterday the boss came up to me and said,
    "What's happened to what's-his-name?"

8   The police arrested Peter at his home yesterday for stealing flowers. Peter claimed that the
    evidence . . . . *(plant)* on him!

9   An arrogant lady . . . . *(show)* round a private art gallery in Paris.
    Standing at the door of the gallery as she was leaving, the woman looked at a modern
    painting of a woman by Picasso and said:
    > I suppose you call this painting a work of art.
    The owner, who . . . . *(annoy)* by the woman's negative
    attitude to his collection, said:
    > No, I call that a mirror.

10 The body of a man was found in a house yesterday. The body . . . .
    (chop) up into a thousand pieces and placed in a large plastic bag. Police have not ruled
    out suicide.

I've never been bitten by a dog. Write some sentences about yourself using the pattern:
    I've never been + past participle.
Have you ever been: *attacked by … , involved in … , arrested for …, involved in a car
accident, run over by … , accused of stealing … , bitten by a … , kissed by …* ?

34   Have something done

Each of the following jokes contains the structure *have something done*. For example: *I've just had my car serviced*. Complete them using the following words:

head	nails	fingers	hair
room	the goal	teeth	Venetian blinds

1   How would you like to have your . . . . cut?
> Just like my dad's. You know – like a doughnut.
What do you mean?
> Leave a hole on the top.

2   One week after he arrived in prison, Walter Gidon had his appendix removed. Soon after that he had two . . . . amputated after an accident in the prison kitchen. The prison boss said to one of the wardens:
> Keep an eye on him. I think he's trying to escape bit by bit.

3   Edward was visiting his friend Angus who was very mean. Edward found Angus watching a man carefully removing the wallpaper from the walls of his living room.
> Are you having the . . . . redecorated? Edward asked.
Of course not, replied Angus. I'm moving house.

4   My dog bit my wife yesterday.
> What did you do?
I took it to the vet.
> Did you have it put to sleep?
Of course not. I had its . . . . sharpened.

5   My mother has finally stopped biting her . . . .
> How did she manage that?
We had all her teeth pulled out.

6   Doctor, I bought a pair of shoes for £500 and my mother says I need to have my . . . . examined, so I've come to see you.
> I'll examine you for £50.
Okay, and if you find the £50, you can keep it.

7   Mrs Murray was having a shower when the doorbell rang.
Who is it? she shouted.
> Blindman, came the reply.
She went downstairs without putting any clothes on.
She opened the door and the man said:
> Where exactly do you want to have these . . . . fitted?

8   Margaret, an accountant, went to a football match with her boyfriend. It was her first football match and she knew nothing about the game. She asked him,
What's the man doing in front of the big net?
> He's the goalkeeper. He has to stop the ball going into the net.
And how much is he paid?
> About £3000 a week.
What! Surely it would be cheaper to have . . . . covered up?

Have you *had anything done* recently? Here are some ideas: *hair cut, house painted, car serviced, the sitting-room re-decorated, a modem installed.* And on a more personal level: *some fillings replaced, eyes tested, some clothes dry-cleaned, nails done, roots done, legs waxed.*

Section Five
Verb Patterns

Grammar or vocabulary?

Traditionally, we have divided the language into grammar and vocabulary. We always knew that some areas were grey – they seemed like grammar, but students just had to learn them. Phrasal verbs are a good example. Most students think of them as part of the grammar of English, but they are fixed verbal expressions. Learning them is more like learning vocabulary.

> You've really got to *face up to* your problems, you know.
> Do you *believe in* life after death?
> I wish you wouldn't *insist on* calling me Pooh in front of my friends!

There are many expressions using verbs which are best treated like vocabulary. In particular, verbs which can be followed by an infinitive structure or a gerund structure fall into this category:

> He *refused to do* his homework.
> I *promised to wash* the car.
> I *persuaded her to invite* you as well.

> Would you *consider offering* him the job?
> I keep *forgetting* his name.

It is much better for students to learn the grammar of the word when they learn the word rather than build this area up into the 'Infinitives or gerunds problem'. Students cannot guess which verb takes which structure. It is something they have to learn through meeting lots of examples. Rules do not help in this area.

35 Verb + infinitive

All the following verbs can be followed by the infinitive (*hope to be able to come*). Complete the jokes using the correct form of the verbs:

hope	*learn*	*try*	*want*	*forget*	*plan*
decide	*need*	*wish*	*refuse*	*promise*	*fail*

1 Why is James sticking his tongue out?
> I guess the doctor . . . . to tell him to put it back in.

2 Your school report is very disappointing. I . . . . to buy you a bicycle if you passed your exams. What have you been doing with your time?
> . . . . to ride a bicycle!

3 Mrs Merton was 45. She was a very vain person and talked a lot about getting old and losing her good looks. At one party, she approached a stranger and said:
> I . . . . to think of my fiftieth birthday.
Why? replied the stranger. What happened?

4 Officer, I . . . . to report a burglary. I'm trapped in an old lady's bedroom.
> Who's calling? asked the policeman.
The burglar.

5 How can I help you, sir?
> Tomorrow I . . . . to catch a late train to London.
Take the 4.30. It's nearly always thirty minutes late.

6 Why did the busy little boy put the calendar in his piggy bank?
> He was . . . . to save time!

7 I . . . . to return this tennis racket.
> Why? What's wrong with it?
I've . . . . to win a single game since I bought it!

8 A man stood at the bar in a pub and said in a loud voice,
I was born an Englishman. I live as an Englishman and I . . . . to die an Englishman.
> Have you no ambition? said a Scotsman sitting in the corner.

9 David was madly in love with June and wanted to marry her. However, he was too shy to ask her face to face so he . . . . to phone her.
> Darling, he said. Will you marry me?
Of course, I will, she replied. Who is speaking?

10 I'm . . . . to become a great actor and to see my name up in lights.
> Then can I suggest you change your name to 'Toilets'?

I hope to become the best footballer in the world.
I plan to sail round the world single-handed.
I'm trying to master kung-fu.
I refuse to get involved in other people's problems.
I promised never to make a speech again.
I've decided to give up sugar.

Now think of some more sentences about your hopes using this pattern: *I hope to ... .*

36   Verb + object + infinitive

These verbs are followed by an object, then an infinitive. (*I taught my son to drive.*) Complete
the jokes with the correct form of these verbs:

     remind   *require*   *order*   *expect*   *teach*
     persuade   *allow*   *warn*   *ask*   *encourage*

1   I . . . . my dog to play chess.
    > That's amazing! It must be very clever.
    Not really. It's only beaten me once so far.

2   An insurance salesman was trying to . . . . Mr Jones to buy a new policy.
    Last week I sold a policy to a man in the next street. Two days later he was run over by
    a bus and lost both legs. We paid him £50,000. Just think, you might be just as lucky!

3   In my hotel I do not . . . . guests to make a noise. Do you have any children?
    > No.
    Do you have any pets?
    > No.
    Any musical instruments?
    > No, but my pen does scratch a little when I write!

4   You . . . . a fishing permit to fish here.
    > Thanks, officer. But I'm doing all right with worms.

5   A customs officer stopped Patrick at the airport
    and . . . . him to open his suitcase.
    > What's in that bottle? asked the officer.
    Holy water from the city of Jerusalem.
    (The officer opened the bottle and tasted it.)
    > This isn't water, shouted the officer. It's wine.
    Praise the Lord! Another miracle! shouted Patrick.

6   You're not supposed to eat with your knife.
    > I know, but how do you . . . .
    me to eat with a fork when it leaks?

7   My Aunt Maureen was very embarrassed last night.
    > What happened?
    She was at a fancy dress party and a man . . . . her to remove her mask.
    > What's embarrassing about that?
    She wasn't wearing one!

8   On the way to the seaside little Johnny saw a lovely new Rolls-Royce. He ran his new
    spade along the side of the car, scratching it badly.
    I . . . . you not to do that, shouted his father.
    > But why, dad?
    Because if you break that spade, you're not getting another one.

9   My father is . . . . me to become a magician and to saw people in half.
    > Do you have any brothers and sisters?
    No, but I have three half-sisters and two half-brothers!

10 The doctor has just . . . . me to take your temperature.
    > Why, nurse? Doesn't he have one of his own?

My parents never *allowed me to stay out* late at night.
What about your parents? *My parents never allowed me to ... .*
If you yourself are a parent, you can start: *I never allow my children to ... .*
If you are not yet a parent, you can start: *I'd never allow my children to ... .*

37 Verb + -ing

Some verbs are often found followed by the -ing form of another verb. (*I admitted having a cigarette.*) Complete the jokes using the correct form of the following verbs:

consider	risk	suggest	keep	admit
advise	enjoy	involve	regret	avoid

1 Doctor, you told me to take these pills on an empty stomach.
> Did they do you any good?
I don't know. They . . . . rolling off!

2 My dog digs holes in my garden all the time. What can I do about it?
> Have you . . . . hiding the spade?

3 Gordon was blind and having trouble with his eyes.
> Doctor, I have developed this strange problem. Every time I have a cup of coffee I get a pain in my right eye.
I . . . . taking the spoon out of the cup before you drink it next time!

4 Can I . . . . drinking the bottled water in this hotel?
> Certainly, sir. The manager has passed all the water himself!

5 Two very young babies are in bed together. One says:
> Are you a boy or a girl?
I don't know.
> I know how to tell. It . . . . looking
under the blanket. Do you want to look?
Okay.
> No doubt about it. You're a girl.
But how can you tell?
> Easy. You've got pink socks and I've got blue ones.

6 Did you know that the people of Prague
. . . . reading books about money?
> Really? What kind of books are they?
Czech books!

7 (*On a bus.*) Please have your tickets ready for inspection.
> I'm sorry, Inspector, but my son has eaten his bus ticket.
Well, madam, may I . . . . buying him a second helping!

8 Doctor, I really . . . . getting this wooden leg. It's giving me a lot of trouble.
> Why is that?
Every day my wife hits me over the head with it!

9 A judge is about to sentence a man who was convicted of dangerous driving.
> As you . . . . driving too fast and causing a serious accident, this court finds you guilty. The sentence is £500 or six months in jail.
Well, I don't have to think too long about that decision, judge. I'll take the £500!

10 Smith, thousands of people are killed each year on British roads. What is the best way to
. . . . having accidents on the road?
> Drive on the pavement, sir?

What do you *enjoy doing* on Sundays? Is there anything in your life you *regret doing*? Are there things you *avoid doing*? What about something you can't *imagine yourself ever doing*?

38   Verb + preposition

Certain verbs are followed by a particular preposition. Complete the jokes below by putting the correct preposition in the gaps provided:

1   Is it really bad luck to have a black cat following you?
> Well, it depends.
What do you mean?
> Well, it depends . . . . . . whether you're a man or a mouse.

2   Two goldfish were swimming around in a bowl.
One said to the other:
> Do you believe . . . . . . God?
Yes, replied the second goldfish. Who do you
think changes the water?

"Do you believe in God?"

3   The president of the football club approached Bob.
> We are looking . . . . . . a treasurer.
But I thought you hired a new treasurer two months ago.
> That's right. That's the treasurer we're looking . . . .

4   You're new, aren't you, boy? What's your name?
> Simon, sir.
In this school we insist . . . . . . surnames. What's your surname, boy?
> Darling, sir.
Er ... All right, Simon. Yours is the desk by the window.

5   Your problem is that you're always wishing . . . . . . something you don't have.
> But what else is there to wish . . . . . . ?

6   So, soldier. You're complaining . . . . . . a little sand in your soup?
> Yes, sir.
Did you join the army to serve your country or to complain . . . . . . the food?
> I joined the army to serve my country, not to eat it, sir.

7   Everyone should have at least two friends.
> Why?
One to talk . . . . . . and one to talk . . . .

8   Why did the cannibal have bad indigestion?
> I don't know.
He ate somebody who disagreed . . . . . . him!

9   Do you approve . . . . . . free speech?
> I certainly do.
Oh good. Can I use your telephone?

10   Mrs Jones, I'm a little worried . . . . . . your son, Bobby. He goes round the school all
day shouting Cluck! Cluck! Cluck! We can't get him to speak, read or write.
> Oh, don't worry, headmaster. Bobby thinks he's a chicken.
But haven't you taken him to a psychologist?
> Well, we would, but we need the eggs!

---

1. What was the last thing you complained *about*?
2. Have you ever eaten anything that disagreed *with* you?
3. Are you worried *about* anything at the moment? What is it?
4. Can you give examples of a few things you believe *in* strongly?

39   Verb + preposition + -*ing*

Complete the jokes below by putting a suitable preposition in the gaps provided:

1   Two of the world's richest men were sitting in a restaurant, trying to impress each other.
> I'm thinking . . . . . . buying all the world's gold mines, boasted one of them.
The other looked thoughtful, then said:
> I'm not so sure I want to sell them!

2   A waiter is bringing the food to Mr Smith's table.
> Waiter! exclaimed Mr Smith. Why have you got your thumb on my steak?
Ah, said the waiter thoughtfully. To prevent it . . . . . . falling off the plate, sir!

3   What did you get your grandfather for his birthday?
> Nothing.
But I thought you were going to get him
some handkerchiefs.
> At the store I decided . . . . . . getting them.
Why?
> Er ... because I couldn't remember what size
his nose was!

4   Mummy, you know that old vase in the hall.
> Yes.
The one that has been handed down from
generation to generation.
> Yes.
Well, this generation has come to apologise . . . . . . dropping it!

5   An employee received £10 too much in his pay-packet but didn't mention it to his boss.
However, the boss eventually noticed his error and the following week he deducted the
ten pounds from the employee's wages.
> Hey, said the employee. I'm £10 short this week.
You didn't say anything last week when you were paid ten pounds too much.
> No, replied the employee. I can forgive you . . . . . . making one mistake, but when it
happens twice, it's time to speak up!

6   I'm not looking forward . . . . . . asking Mr Smith for his daughter's hand.
> Why don't you ask for all of her?

7   Sherlock Holmes, the famous detective, called one morning on his assistant, Dr Watson.
> Watson, why are you wearing red underwear today?
Amazing, Holmes! I must congratulate you . . . . . . detecting the colour of my
underwear. But tell me, how do you do it?
> Elementary, my dear Watson! You've forgotten to put your trousers on.

8   Harry kept returning to the ticket office in the cinema.
That's the sixth ticket you've bought for the same film, sir. Is there a problem?
> There sure is. There's a girl inside who insists . . . . . . tearing them up!

9   Prisoner, this court has accused you . . . . . . stealing £5,000 but it has been unable to
prove you guilty. Therefore, you are now free to go. Do you have anything to say?
> Does that mean I can keep the money?

I've always dreamed of living in a castle / retiring / meeting the right person.
Write similar sentences about what you *have always dreamed of doing.*

40 Expressions + -ing

Complete these jokes by putting *point, use, worth,* **or** *waste* **in the gaps provided:**

1   Alan and Bob were in a restaurant. They had been waiting for thirty minutes to be
    served. Bob snapped his fingers to get some service.
    > It's not . . . . trying to attract a waiter's attention in this restaurant. The
    waiters are so proud and arrogant that they decide when to come and serve you.
    But that's ridiculous!
    Thirty minutes later, Bob stood up and shouted at a waiter:
    > Waiter. What do I have to do to get a glass of water in this place?
    The waiter looked disdainfully at Bob and said:
    > Set yourself on fire, sir!

2   When Helen was visiting an old aunt she had not seen for
    years, she saw a parrot on a perch in the corner of the room.
    > Oh, what a lovely parrot you've got. Hello, Polly. Who's
    a pretty boy, then. Hello, Polly.
    It's no . . . . talking to that parrot.
    > Why? joked Helen. Is it tongue-tied?
    No, said the aunt. It's stuffed!

3   Bobby: You're impossible, Claire. It's a . . . .
             of time talking to you. You're so stupid.
    Dad: Stop upsetting your little sister. Say you're sorry.
    Bobby: OK. Claire?
    Claire: What?
    Bobby: I'm sorry you're stupid!

4   A lady has arrived at a hotel and is talking to the manager:
    > I like to relax when I'm on holiday. So for me, it's not . . . . staying in a hotel
    if it's noisy. Now, are your rooms quiet?
    Of course they are, madam. It's the people inside them who are noisy!

5   A commuter was extremely angry because his morning train was frequently late. He
    decided that it was time to complain, so he went to the station manager.
    > What's the . . . . in having a timetable if the trains are never on time? he asked.
    The manager thought for a moment, then said:
    > Well, how would you know the trains were late if there wasn't a timetable!

6   For goodness sake! You are SO stupid. It's a . . . . of time trying to explain it to
    you. You're the closest thing to a complete idiot!
    > Oh! So you want me to move away from you, do you?

7   A boy fell from a tree and hit his head. In the ambulance, the doctor asked him his name:
    > What's your name, young man?
    Why? asked the boy.
    > So that we can tell your family.
    But there's no . . . . in doing that. They already know my name!

8   A giant American car sped into a sleepy English village. The driver rolled down his
    window and shouted to a villager:
    > Tell me. Am I on the right road to William Shakespeare's house?
    Yes, but there's little . . . . in hurrying to get there.
    > Why?
    He's dead! He died years ago.

There's no point in taking an umbrella to Egypt because it never rains.
Can you write more sentences following this pattern: *There's no point in ... because ... .*

41 Make / let

Complete the jokes below by using *make* or *let*:

1 Yesterday I went to the doctor about my bad memory.
   > What did he do?
   He . . . . me pay in advance.

2 Why are you always angry when you travel by ferry?
   > Because every time I get on one, it . . . . me cross.

3 When I was eight months old, I could walk.
   > You think you're clever. When I was that age, I . . . . them carry me.

4 Jack and Dick saw two men fishing in a most peculiar way. One of the men was holding
   the other by the ankles and the second was hanging over the bridge catching the fish with
   his hands. They had caught a lot of fish and every couple of minutes the man hanging
   over the bridge would throw another one up on to the road. "Let's try that!" said Jack,
   so off they walked till they found another bridge. Dick held on to Jack's ankles and
   waited for his friend to start throwing up fish. Five minutes passed and they had caught
   nothing ... ten minutes, twenty minutes, an hour, two hours, and still no fish. Suddenly
   Jack shouted, "Quick, Dick, don't . . . . . . go! Pull me up! There's a train coming!"

"There's a train coming!"

5 How do you . . . . a hat talk?
   > I don't know.
   Add the letter C and you . . . . it chat!

6 Alan, you remind me of the sea.
   > You mean, you find me wild and romantic?
   No, it's because you . . . . me sick.

7 When are your eyes not eyes?
   > I don't know.
   When the wind . . . . them water.

8 What do seven days of dieting do to you?
   > I don't know.
   They . . . . one weak.

9 I've decided to . . . . my hair grow.
   > But how can you stop it?

10 Dad, I want to get married.
   > And who do you have in mind?
   Grandmother.
   > You don't think I'd . . . . you marry my mother, do you?
   Why not? said the little boy. You married mine.

11 Helen was saying her prayers.
   Please God . . . . the French change the capital of France from Paris to Lyon.
   > Helen, her mother said. Why do you want God to . . . . the French change their
   capital city?
   Because that's what I wrote in my Geography exam!

When I was a child my parents *made me brush my teeth* night and morning. They never *let
me eat sweets* in bed or *watch TV* after 8 at night.

What do / did your parents make you do / never make you do?
What do / did they let you do / never let you do?

Section Six

Articles etc

Determiners

This section deals with that area known as determiners – articles *(a/an, the)*, quantifiers *(some, any, a few etc)*, possessives *(my, your etc)* – the words which come in front of nouns and before adjectives.

Some and any

We used to give students the simple but misleading rule: use *some* in positive statements and *any* in negative statements and questions. This reduced the problem to a structural one when the real problem was the difference in meaning between *some* and *any*.

Some is used to talk about a restricted quantity or amount:

> I've got *some* very nice friends. I'm very lucky.
> I know *some* people who never vote.
> I don't like *some* modern music.

Any is used when the quantity or amount is unrestricted:

> He doesn't have *any* friends. He's so difficult.
> I don't know *anyone* who doesn't vote Labour.
> I don't like *any* modern music.

Countable and uncountable nouns

Some determiners depend on whether the following noun is countable or uncountable. For example:

Countable nouns use *many* and *a few*:

I don't take *many days* off.   I had *a few days* off last month.

Uncountable nouns use *much* and *little*:

It didn't take *much time* to finish it off.   I have very *little* free *time* at the moment.

a lot of / lots of

A lot of and *lots of* tend to be used in positive statements, but they can also be used after *not:*

We've had *a lot of* complaints recently.
Have you got much money on you? > *Not a lot.*

42 Some / any

Complete the jokes below by using *some* or *any* in the gaps provided:

1 Waiter, I'd like . . . . coffee. Why isn't there . . . . on the menu?
> Because I wiped it off.

2 Do you have . . . . holes in your socks?
> Of course not.
Then how do you get your feet into them?

3 Do you have. . . . . cheap rooms?
> Sure, but you have to make your own bed.
I'll take one!
> Right. Here's a hammer, ... nails and . . . . wood.

4 There aren't . . . . flies in the kitchen today. How did you manage that?
> Easy! I put the rubbish bin in the living-room!

5 Are you married?
> Yes.
Do you have . . . . . . children?
> Six boys and two girls.
Eight children altogether. That's fantastic!
> Not really. I had them one at a time.

6 Andrew! Did you eat . . . . biscuits when I was out last night?
> I didn't touch one!
Well, there was a full packet in the cupboard when I left. Now there's only one left.
> That's the one I didn't touch!

7 There will be no ice-cream until you wash your hands.
> But I DID wash my hands.
You didn't use . . . . soap or water.
> Well, haven't you heard of dry-cleaning?

8 Doctor, I need . . . . advice. I seem to get fat in certain places. What can I do?
> Stay away from those places!

9 A man went into a pet shop.
> Can I help you, sir? asked the shop assistant.
Yes. Do you have . . . . dogs going cheap?
> I'm sorry, sir. All our dogs go "Woof! Woof!"

10 *(At the butcher's)*
I'd like . . . . steak and make it lean.
> Certainly, madam. Which way should I make it lean, left or right?

I don't have any brothers or sisters.
Write some sentences about yourself with the pattern: *I don't have any ... .*

43   Much / many / a lot of

Complete the jokes using *much, many,* or *a lot of*:

1   We don't have . . . . beautiful women in our town.
     > Why do you say that?
     Well, we had a beauty contest and nobody won!

2   How . . . . money do you have in the bank?
     > I don't know. I haven't shaken it recently.

3   John is so stupid. He thinks a football coach has four wheels.
     > Well, how . . . . wheels does it have?

4   Taxi driver, I haven't got . . . . money. What's the fare to the railway station?
     > Five pounds, sir.
     Oh! And how . . . . for my large suitcase?
     > Fifty pence, sir.
     Right. Take my suitcase to the station. I'll walk.

5   A horse walked into a bar and said to the barman,
     Same as usual, Sam.
     > Look, said the barman. I serve . . . .
     customers in this bar every day. How do you
     expect me to remember what they all drink!

6   What do you take for a headache?
     > I drink . . . . beer the night before!

7   I don't have . . . . hair and I'd like to buy a wig.
     > Certainly, sir. That's £50 plus tax.
     Forget the tacks. I'll use glue.

8   Ten blackbirds are sitting on a wall and the farmer shoots one of them with his gun.
     How . . . . are left?
     > None, sir.
     What do you mean?
     > Well, the other birds flew away!

9   How . . . . do you know about 18th-century English scientists?
     > Nothing. They're all dead!

10   Why are . . . . artists Italian?
     > I don't know.
     Because they were born in Italy!

I don't have many friends. I don't have much spare time. I've got a lot of work this week.
Write some more sentences about yourself using this pattern:
I don't have many / much ... . I've got a lot of ... .

44 A few / a little

Complete the jokes below using *a few* or *a little*:

1 Doctor! Help me quickly! I think I'm shrinking.
   > Well, first you will have to learn to be . . . . patient!

2 That will be £20, sir.
   > That's a lot of money for a haircut, especially as I'm going bald and I only have
   . . . . hairs.
   That's the trouble, sir. It's the time I spent finding the hairs that cost the money!

3 Why is there only . . . . honey in Brazil?
   > Because there is only one 'B' in Brazil.

4 There were quite . . . . cakes in the cupboard last night when I went out. Now
   there's only one left. Why is that, John?
   > I didn't put the light on so I missed it!

5 This match won't light.
   > Why? What's wrong with it?
   I don't know. It was all right . . . . minutes ago.

6 Carol is sitting alone in a restaurant. A man leaves his
   table and comes over to her table.
   > Would you like . . . . company?
   Why? Do you have one to sell?

7 Did you hear about the butcher who accidentally sat
   on his bacon slicer?
   > No, what happened?
   He got . . . . behind in his orders!

8 Most girls think that I'm handsome but
   . . . . girls think I'm ugly.
   What do you think, Julie?
   > A bit of both.
   What exactly do you mean?
   > I think you're pretty ugly!

9 Who is bigger, Mr Bigger, Mrs Bigger or baby Bigger?
   > Mr Bigger, I suppose.
   No. The baby because it's . . . . Bigger!

10 Paul's girlfriend was very beautiful. However, she was deaf. On her birthday Paul sent
   her a very expensive bird. It was a very colourful parrot which could sing in English and
   recite poetry. The following day he called at his girlfriend's flat and asked:
   > What did you think of the bird?
   It was . . . . tough when I took it out of the oven, she said with a smile,
   so I boiled it with . . . . herbs and it was delicious.

---

1. Only a few.
2. Just a little.
Work with a partner. Take turns to try to make each other respond using one of these
answers. Here are some questions to get you started: *Have you ever smoked cigars? Do you
ever drink black coffee? Have you a lot of friends? Have you lots of relations? How many
girl/boy friends have you had? How much money have you got in your wallet?*

45 Some / any / no / every

Complete the jokes below using one of the following:

something	*nothing*	*anything*
nobody	*everybody*	*anywhere*

1 There's . . . . I can do that . . . . else in my school can do. Not even the teachers!
> What's that?
Read my handwriting!

2 Welcome on board flight DB 123 to London. You are flying on a computerised aircraft without a pilot. Don't worry. . . . . can go wrong. . . . . can go wrong. . . . . can go wrong. . . . . can go wrong.

3 Doctor, ... ignores me.
> Next, please!

4 What a strange world! . . . . wants to go to Heaven, but . . . . wants to die!

5 What flies all day without going . . . .?
> A flag.

6 You're fired!
> But I haven't done . . . .
That's why you've just lost your job.

7 I saw . . . . last night that I will never get over.
> What?
The moon.

"Welcome on board. This is your computer speaking."

8 Mrs Clark went out for the day. She left a note on the door for the milkman.
. . . . AT HOME – DON'T LEAVE . . . .
When she got home the door of the house was open. There was a new note on the door.
It said: THANKS. WE HAVEN'T LEFT . . . .!

9 Where does the heavyweight boxing champion of the world sit when he goes to the cinema?
> I don't know.
. . . . he wants!

10 Why are you crawling into my classroom, Billy?
> I'm just doing what you told us to do, sir!
What do you mean?
> Well, on the first day you said . . . . ever walked into your classroom late.

---

1. Work in pairs and ask each other about the following problems using the pattern below:
sore head, toothache, a cold, sore feet, an upset stomach, a bad back, etc.
   Can you recommend something for a sore throat?
   > Yes, I always get some lemon sweets from the chemists.

2. Work again in pairs and discuss the kind of thing you never eat and the kind of things you love eating, using *anything*.
   I never eat anything with sugar in it.   I'll eat anything sweet!

Complete the jokes using one of the following words:

weather   furniture   information   progress
traffic   scenery   advice   luggage

1   Do you have any . . . . , sir?
    > Yes, I'd like this small bag to go to Moscow and I'd like the large bag to go to New York. I'd also like my suitcase to go to Paris.
    > But sir, Beranti Airlines can't do that!
    Why not? You did it last month when I flew with you.

2   Fred's father is giving him a driving lesson.
    > When we join the . . . . on the main road, remember just one thing, son.
    What's that, Dad?
    > If you're going to hit something, hit something cheap!

3   I've just finished a course about how to make decisions and I've made a lot of . . . . I think I've finally been cured of my indecision.
    > That's great.
    At least I think I have.

4   Dr Freud, a famous psychiatrist, was meeting a new patient.
    > As this is your first visit and I have no . . . . about you, I suggest that you start at the very beginning and describe your problem.
    Well, doctor, in the beginning I created Heaven and Hell, the earth, the sea and ...

"Why not start at the beginning?"

5   What is something everybody gives but nobody takes?
    > I don't know.
    . . . .

6   A man went into a shop to buy some . . . .
    > I'd like to buy a mattress, he said to the shop assistant.
    A spring mattress, sir?
    > No. I'd like one I can use all year round.

7   Eve fell out of a window when she was on holiday. She was admiring the . . . .
    > But that's terrible! Was she badly injured?
    No, she was staying in a bungalow.

8   What terrible . . . . ! This heat is getting me down.
    > Why don't you throw the thermometer out of the window?
    Why?
    > Because there would be an instant drop in the temperature!

I'd like some information about holidays in Antarctica. Make up some true sentences about yourself with the pattern: *I'd like some information about ... .*

47 Possessives

Complete these jokes by putting *my* or *mine*, *your* or *yours*, *his*, *her* or *hers*, *its*, *our* or *ours*, *their* or *theirs*, in the gaps provided:

1 I'm afraid Alice will not be at school today.
> Who's calling?
It's . . . . . . mother.

2 John and George, is this . . . . . . football?
> Did it break anything, sir?
No, not that I know of.
> Then yes, sir, it's . . . .

3 That's a nice dog you have. What's . . . . . . name?
> I don't know. It won't tell me.

4 Last week a man stole a pair of trousers
from my uncle's shop.
> Did your uncle chase the thief?
No, they were . . . . . . trousers.

5 A man walked into a shop and said:
> I'd like some really tight jeans, please.
Certainly, sir. Will you walk this way?
> If the jeans are as tight as . . . . . .
I'll probably have to!

6 Is that Susan's brother?
> Yes.
He's very small, isn't he?
> Well, he's only . . . . . . half-brother.

"Will you walk this way?"

7 Two boys went into a café and began to eat . . . . . . sandwiches.
> You can't eat . . . . . . own food here, shouted the waiter.
The boys smiled at each other, then they swapped sandwiches.

8 Miss, I can't find . . . . . . shoes anywhere.
> There's one pair left outside the classroom. Are you sure they aren't . . . . . . ?
Yes, I'm sure. . . . . . . had snow on them.

9 Mary and I want to get married but we can't find anywhere to live.
> Why don't you stay with Mary's parents?
Because they're still living with . . . . . . parents!

10 My husband puts his money in the bank. What does your husband do with . . . . . . ?
> He puts it in oil.
What a stupid thing to do! Who wants oily money!

I'd like my own room but I have too many brothers and sisters.
Talk about yourself with this pattern:
I'd like my own ... but ...

48 Reflexive Pronouns

Complete the jokes using these reflexive pronouns:

myself   *yourself*   *himself*   *herself*   *ourselves*   *themselves*

1   A karate champion joined the army and nearly killed . . . . the first time he saluted an officer.

2   Do you believe in life after death?
    > No, but two of my best friends must believe in reincarnation. In their wills they have left everything to . . . .

3   What did you think of my mother's cake?
    > Oh, I thought it was wonderful. Did she buy it . . . . ?

4   Teacher: Your son almost got a black eye today, Mrs Smith.
    Parent: Oh, what happened?
    Teacher: I controlled . . . .

5   My husband is very upset about his weight.
    > Why?
    Yesterday he decided to weigh . . . .
    so he stood on the talking weighing-
    machine in the town centre.
    > What did it say?
    One at a time, please!

6   Why are you scratching . . . . ?
    > Because only I know where I itch!

7   I'd like a first class stamp, please.
    > There you are. That's 26 pence.
    Do I stick the stamp on . . . . ?
    > No. You stick it on the envelope.

"One at a time, please!"

8   Did you write this poem . . . . ?
    > Every line of it, sir.
    Well, I'm very glad to meet you, Mr William Shakespeare. I thought you were dead!

9   Well, for a 110-ten-year-old man and a 115-year-old woman, you are both in very good condition. What's your secret?
    > We keep . . . . fit through regular exercise, doctor.
    What kind of exercise do you take?
    > Well, every Saturday we walk ten miles to watch our dad play football.

10 I've come to tune your piano, sir.
    > I always do that . . . . Who asked you to come?
    Your neighbours!

Do you like the room? I did it *myself*.
Have you been in Mary's car? She fixed it *herself*. She even re-sprayed it *herself*!

Talk about things you've done yourself or a friend has done himself / herself. For example:
paint the sitting-room, fix your computer, install more memory in your computer, wash your windows, bake a cake, make a delicious meal for your friends, etc.

Section Seven
Adjectives and Adverbs

Adjectives

Several units in this section focus on adjectival expressions:

adjectives with a preposition:	*proud of*
adjectives with an infinitive:	*good to eat*

It helps students if they can make lists of different adjectives which take the same preposition. For example:

WITH	*bored with, satisfied with, pleased with, content with*
OF	*proud of, afraid of, tired of, jealous of, ashamed of*

This is an area where students must simply learn the expressions. There are no short cuts or rules.

Order of adjectives

This is an area where there are some rules, but the rules are so difficult to apply that it is best for students to meet lots of different examples and try to develop a 'feel' for what sounds right.

Comparatives and superlatives

Some two-syllable adjectives worry students. They have learned the rule that with longer adjectives we use *more* or *most – more difficult, most interesting*. They then meet *commoner* and *more common* and they sometimes come across *more* or *most* used with monosyllabic adjectives where a native speaker is using them to give emphasis. For example:

Which is better – this example or that one?
> I'm not sure. This one is *much more pure*.

'purer' would also have been correct, but for some reason of emphasis the native speaker chose *more pure!*

Decide which is correct in the following: the adjective ending in -*ed* or in -*ing*:

1   Why are you looking so *depressed / depressing*?
    > I've just been to the doctor and he told me I would have to take a pill every day for the rest of my life.
    Why is that so *depressed / depressing*?
    > He only gave me twenty-five pills.

2   How many sheep do you think are in this field? a farmer asked his new assistant.
    > Four hundred and sixty, the assistant replied in seconds.
    That's *astonished / astonishing*! You're perfectly correct. How did you do it?
    > Oh, there's no need to be *astonished / astonishing*, the assistant said. It's quite simple really. You just count the number of legs and divide by four.

3   A man went into a new fruit shop in London which sold fruit from all over the world. He picked some oranges but he was *shocked / shocking* when the shop assistant asked him for £9.50. He gave the girl a £10 note and said, "Your prices are *shocked / shocking*." Then he left the shop. The assistant ran after him and said, "Sir, you've forgotten your change." The man turned round and said sarcastically, "Oh, you'd better keep it. I stood on a grape on the way out!"

4   I was extremely *embarrassed / embarrassing* yesterday. I called my wife Sue.
    > What's *embarrassed / embarrassing* about that?
    Her name's Edwina!

5   Mary: That boy over there is *annoyed / annoying* me.
    Jane: But he is not even looking at you.
    Mary: That's what I am *annoyed / annoying* about!

6   My husband's trip to the Grand Canyon was extremely *disappointed / disappointing*. His face fell when he got off the bus.
    > Why? Was he *disappointed / disappointing* with the view?
    No, he fell over the edge.

7   Alan Wilson was an extremely *irritated / irritating* person who talked for hours about himself. At one party he was talking proudly about his travels.
    > Yes, I've hunted in North America and South America. I've hunted across New Zealand and Australia. I've hunted all over India and Africa.
    Oh! asked an *irritated / irritating* old lady. What on earth have you lost?

8   I've got an *amazed / amazing* watch. It only cost me £1.
    > Why is it *amazed / amazing*?
    Because every time I look at it I'm *amazed / amazing* it's still working.

I failed my driving test. *I was very disappointed.*
I paid £100 for dinner. *The food was extremely disappointing.*
Use the adjectives from the jokes to talk about yourself and things you have experienced:

    amazed / amazing   *irritated / irritating*   *disappointed / disappointing*
    annoyed / annoying   *shocked / shocking*   *embarrassed / embarrassing*

50 Adjective + preposition

Some adjectives are followed by a particular preposition. Complete the jokes by putting a suitable preposition in the gaps provided:

1   I'm proud . . . . . . my husband. He's just become a bank manager.
> I'm ashamed . . . . . . my husband.
Why?
> Because he looks like an ape. When we go
to the zoo he has to buy two tickets.
Why?
> One ticket to get in and one to get out!

2   Did you take my advice and visit my doctor?
> Yes, but I wasn't very impressed . . . . . . him.
Why?
> Well, the first thing he examined was my wallet!

3   Dad, I'm homesick.
> But this is your home, son!
I know. I'm sick . . . . . . it.

4   What kind of ant is good . . . . . . counting?
> An accountANT!

5   I'm sorry to say, Mr Jackson, there's nothing wrong . . . . . . you. You are just lazy.
> Can you give me the medical name for this condition, doctor?
Why?
> So that I can tell my boss why I am not at work.

6   Graham was driving his friend along a very narrow mountain road. After a while his
friend said:
> I'm really frightened . . . . . . the sharp bends in this road.
Then do what I do, replied Graham. Close your eyes as we go round them!

7   Doctor, I'm worried . . . . . . my figure. I've put on three kilos in the last month.
> Well, you'll just have to diet.
What colour?

8   An old man was crawling about the floor of a cinema. The lady in the next seat was
getting very angry . . . . . . him.
> What's your problem? she asked.
I've dropped the toffee I was eating, said the man.
> Why can't you leave it to the end of the film?
Because my false teeth are stuck to it!

9   Excuse me, madam. Would you be interested . . . . . . some orange soap?
> No, thanks. I never wash my oranges.

10   Henry was very disappointed . . . . . . the cup of coffee his wife brought to him in bed.
> This coffee tastes awful.
I don't understand it, said his wife. It's fresh. I made it in my dressing gown.
> No wonder it tastes funny!

Using the jokes above, add the prepositions to the following:

good	frightened	worried	interested ....
disappointed	proud	impressed	sick ....

Now use these phrases to talk about yourself.

51 Adjective + infinitive

Complete the jokes below by putting one of the following adjectives in the gaps provided:

polite	relieved	important	glad
good	shocked	sorry	pleased

1   Dad, are cockroaches . . . . to eat?
    > Don't be stupid. Why do you ask?
    Because there was one in your sandwich!

2   Wilson, your hands are very dirty.
    > I'm sorry, sir.
    What would you say if I came to school with dirty hands?
    > I'd be too . . . . to mention it, sir!

3   I bumped into an old girlfriend in the High Street
    yesterday.
    > And was she . . . . to see you?
    Not really. We were both in our cars at the time!

4   I'm . . . . to be back at work. My holiday was awful. It rained every day.
    > But where did you get the wonderful tan?
    That's not a tan. It's rust!

5   Good morning, Mr Abbot. How are you after your heart operation?
    > Fine, doctor. You seem to have done a good job. However, there is one small problem.
    And what is that?
    > I seem to have two heartbeats.
    Oh, I'm . . . . to hear that. Now I know where my Rolex is!

6   I'm . . . . to tell you that you have a very serious disease. I'm afraid it's
    rabies. You'll probably be dead within a week. There's nothing I can do.
    > Well, doctor, give me a pen and a piece of paper.
    Why? Are you going to write your will?
    > No, I'm going to make a list of all the people I want to bite!

7   I was . . . . to read in the newspaper that one in four people today are
    mentally ill.
    > I know. It's worrying. If three of your friends are all right, then it must be you!

8   Soldier! In the army it is extremely . . . . to be able to tell where you are.
    > Yes, sir!
    Now, imagine you are facing north. East is on your right and west is on your left. What is
    behind you, soldier?
    > My backpack, sir?

Here are some more adjectives which can be followed by the *to*-infinitive:

able	unwilling	prepared	willing
likely	unable	afraid	happy

Can you say some true things about yourself, using those adjectives and the ones used in the
jokes above?

52 Too / enough

Cross out the wrong answer in the following. The first has been done for you.

1   Were the peppers *too hot* / ~~hot enough~~, darling?
    > No, dear, smoke always comes out of my ears when I eat.

2   Why aren't Jamaicans growing bananas any longer?
    > I've no idea.
    Because they are *too long / long enough* already.

3   A woman went to a fortune-teller who charged £50 for two questions.
    > Don't you think £50 is *too expensive / expensive enough* for two questions?
    Yes, it is, agreed the fortune-teller. Now what is your second question?

4   When I was younger, I couldn't walk for a whole year.
    > That's terrible. Why was that?
    I wasn't *too old / old enough*.

5   What's a caterpillar?
    > A worm *too rich / rich enough* to own a fur coat.

6   What did the big chimney say to the little chimney?
    > I don't know.
    You're *too young / young enough* to smoke.

7   I like this dog but its legs are *too short / short enough*.
    > What do you mean? They reach the ground, don't they?

8   I'll never pass the exam. I'm not *too clever / clever enough*.
    > I'll sell you some clever pills. That's how I pass exams.
    How much?
    > Two for £5.
    (Buys two and eats them.)
    Hey! These aren't pills, they're sweets.
    > See! They're working already.

9   They put me in jail because I was making big money.
    > What's wrong with that?
    The money was about a centimetre *too big / big enough*.

10 A high-speed lift went from the 25th floor of a new office building to the ground floor in ten seconds and stopped very suddenly.
    > Sorry. Was the stop *too quick / quick enough* for you, sir? said the liftboy to the one man in the lift.
    Oh no, he replied. I usually wear my trousers round my ankles!

Can you finish these sentences in ways that are true for you?

I'm not rich enough to ...   *I'm not strong enough to ...*
I'm not daft enough to ...   *I'm not old enough to ...*
I'm too young to ...   *I'm too inexperienced to ...*
I'm too old to ...   *I'm too sensible to ...*

53 Adverbs

Complete the jokes by placing the following adverbs in the gaps provided:

instantly	*slowly*	*well*	*politely*
atrociously	*fluently*	*perfectly*	*thoroughly*
accurately	*dismissively*	*fast*	*firmly*

1   I said to the dentist that £30 was a lot of money for pulling out a tooth. After all, it only takes five seconds.
> What did he say?
Nothing, he just pulled the tooth out very very . . . . !

2   A small cat was taking her kittens for a walk when a large aggressive cat approached them.
> Woof! Woof! shouted the small cat and the large cat turned away.
See how important it is to speak another language . . . . , the cat said to her kittens.

3   Mrs MacIntosh was a very tidy person. She had just finished cleaning her house . . . . when she heard her son arriving home from school.
> Don't come into the kitchen unless your feet are clean, she shouted.
Her son was already in the kitchen and shouted back:
> My feet are clean, mum. It's my shoes that are dirty.

4   Bill's Mum sent him to buy 3 kilos of apples but he only had two kilos when he got home. His mother phoned the shopkeeper and said:
> I sent my son for 3 kilos of apples but you have only given him two. Did you weigh the fruit . . . . ?
I did. Very carefully! Have you weighed your son?

5   Excuse me, is this spray good for mosquitoes?
> Certainly not, sir. It kills them . . . .

6   What do you do if an elephant sneezes?
> Get out of the way . . . . !

7   My new secretary spells . . . .
> She must be good. I can't spell that.

8   I've got a new hearing aid.
> Does it work . . . . ?
I think it's about three o'clock.

9   Thomas was the ideal child. He always behaved . . . . and every time he was good his mother patted him . . . . on the head and gave him 5 pence. When he was 18 years old, Thomas had £15,000 in the bank but he was only one metre tall.

10   A very short young man walked up to a woman on the dance floor and asked . . . . :
> May I have the pleasure of the next dance?
The woman looked at him and said . . . . :
> I can't dance with a child.
Oh, said the young man. I'm sorry. I wasn't aware of your condition.

Say some true things about yourself by adding an adverb to the following:

I write ...   *I spell ...*   *I sing ...*   *I sleep ...*   *I dance ...*
I speak English ...   *I write English ...*   *I read English ...*

Complete the jokes below using *always, often, sometimes, never* or *usually*. Sometimes more than one is possible:

1   Where can you . . . . find happiness?
> I don't know.
In a dictionary.

2   I've never flown before and I'm a bit afraid. Do these planes . . . . crash?
> Only once!

3   Doctor, when I'm tired I . . . . see
two of everything.
> Sit on the sofa, please.
Which one?

4   What question can . . . . be answered by Yes?
> I don't know.
Are you asleep?

5   Do you write with your left hand or your right hand?
> With my left hand.
Really! I . . . . write with a pencil.

6   You're Peter, aren't you? I . . . . forget a face.
> It's George, actually.
Who said anything about names?

7   Mr Armstrong knows a lot of rude songs.
> But I . . . . hear him singing them in the office.
I know. He . . . . whistles them!

8   Why do you . . . . answer a question with a question?
> Why not?

9   I didn't come here for you to insult me.
> Really! Where do you . . . . go?

10   Football player: Coach, why do all the other players call me Cinderella?
Football coach: Because you . . . . miss the ball!

Make true statements about yourself or someone you know:

IN WINTER:	I sometimes ...	I never ...	I always ...
IN SUMMER:	I always ...	I usually ...	I regularly ...
AT WORK:	I never ...	I always try to ...	
ON HOLIDAY:	I usually ...	I never ...	

55 Order of Adjectives

Put the adjectives in brackets in the correct order in these jokes:

1 *(dead, blue, big)*
Waiter, there's a . . . . fly in this meat soup.
> That's the meat, sir!

2 *(intelligent, young, nice)*
Do you think you could spend your life with a . . . . man like me?
> Sure – as long as he wasn't too much like you!

3 *(thick, library, English)*
I borrowed a . . . . book called "How to Hug" yesterday.
> Are you enjoying it?
No. It was disappointing. I took it back to the library this morning.
> What was wrong with it?
The book was volume 7 of the Encyclopedia Britannica!

4 *(plastic, small, black)*
Doctor, my hair has started to fall out. Can you give me something for it?
> Certainly. Here's a . . . . bag.

5 *(brown, horrible, little)*
Hey! What's that . . . .
thing on your shoulder?
> Aaaaargh! What is it?
Don't panic! It's only your head!

6 *(Italian, red, fast)*
(silk, evening, £2000)
I've got this terrible problem.
> What's wrong?
Well, I've got a . . . . sports car and I've just bought a
. . . . dress for my girlfriend.
> So, what's the problem?
I haven't got any money to pay for them!

7 *(chocolate, home-made, delicious)*
What do you have in your bag?
> Some . . . . cakes.
If I guess how many you've got in your bag, will you give me one?
> Certainly. In fact, if you guess correctly, I'll give you both.
OK. I think you've got six in the bag.

8 *(Spanish, expensive, acoustic)*
Your Uncle Ted is coming tomorrow. Where's the . . . . guitar
he gave you for your birthday?
> I threw it out.
But why? It must have cost him a fortune!
> It had a hole in it!

Can you think of things you can describe using three adjectives? For example: *chilled Italian white wine, pure Scotch malt whisky, fresh wild Scottish salmon, smelly old football boots.*

56   Comparatives

Complete these jokes by putting the adjectives below in the gaps provided. Make sure you use the correct comparative form. For example: *faster; more intelligent.*

fast	*old*	*cheap*	*far*	*intelligent*
light	*big*	*long*	*beautiful*	

1   It's . . . . than a feather but you can't hold it for . . . . than three minutes. What is it?
> I don't know.
Your breath!

2   Would you say the princess is pretty?
> Let's just say she looks . . . . on the radio than she does on television.

3   A lion was running towards two photographers. One of the photographers started to change into his running shoes.
> Don't be ridiculous, said the other photographer. A lion can run at a speed of 50 kilometres an hour.
I'm not interested in the lion. As long as I can run . . . . than you, it doesn't matter!

4   What gets . . . . when you turn it upside down?
> I don't know.
The number 6!

5   A woodpecker was talking to a chicken one day.
> Woodpeckers are very clever birds, it said.
Nonsense, said the chicken. What's clever about banging your head against a tree all day?
Chickens are much . . . . than woodpeckers.
> Really? replied the woodpecker. Have you ever heard of Kentucky Fried Woodpecker!

6   Mr Smith, an American, was not enjoying married life. He was talking to a close friend who was thinking of getting married.
> Take my advice, Mr Smith said. Don't get married. Buy a dog instead.
That's a strange thing to say. Why?
> Because a dog is . . . . than a wife and it already has a fur coat.

7   Which is . . . . away – the moon or Australia?
> Australia, sir.
Why do you say that?
> Well, you can see the moon, but you can't see Australia.

8   Aren't you the same boy who applied for this job three months ago?
Yes, sir.
Didn't I tell you that I wanted an . . . . boy?
Yes, sir. That's why I've come back today.

Can you finish these sentences about yourself:
I'm taller than ...   *I'm younger than ...*   *I'm fitter than ...*
I'm not more intelligent than ...   *I'm more difficult to please than ...*

57 As . . . . as . . . .

Complete the jokes below by putting one of the following words in the gaps provided:

fast	high	hot	hard	beautiful
big	far	safe	long	strong

1   A drunk man was sitting in a restaurant. He called the waiter.
  > Waiter, I can't eat this sandwich. I simply can't get my teeth into it. The bread is as
  . . . . as rock.
  I haven't brought your sandwich yet, sir. You're chewing the tablemat!

2   My dog can jump as . . . . as our house.
  > I don't believe it.
  Why not? Our house can't jump at all.

3   What's as . . . . as an elephant but
  doesn't weigh anything?
  > I don't know.
  Its shadow!

4   I firmly believe that eating meat is good for you. I've eaten
  meat all my life and I'm as . . . . as an ox.
  > That's funny. I've eaten fish all my life and I can't swim at all.

5   How would you describe winter?
  > Well, it's the season when you try to keep your house as
  . . . . as it was in the summer.

6   Brian! Don't reach across the dinner table for the sugar. Use your tongue!
  But mum, my tongue isn't as . . . . as my arm!

7   My little brother is one year old and he can walk across the park by himself.
  > My dog is one year old and it can walk twice as . . . . as your brother.
  That's not surprising. It's got twice as many legs!

8   Dad, do you think I'm vain?
  > No, I don't think so. Why do you ask?
  Because most girls as . . . . as I am, are vain.

9   What do you take for a headache?
  > Nothing acts as . . . . as aspirin.
  Yes, that's why I take nothing!

10 A man was crossing a large field when he suddenly realised that there was a large bull in
  the middle of it. He shouted to the farmer who was standing by the gate:
  > Is that bull dangerous?
  The farmer looked at the bull and said:
  > Let me put it this way. You aren't as . . . . as the bull!

Can you complete these common expressions using this structure:

as quick as *lightning*	as old as the	as green as . . . .
as black as	as white as	as cold as . . . .
as light as a	as good as	as free as a . . . .

58 Superlatives

Complete the jokes below by putting one of the following adjectives in the gaps provided. Make sure you change the adjective to its superlative form: *the oldest, the most delicious.*

old	easy	common	good	quick
small	lazy	delicious	long	large

1   Excuse me, do you know . . . . way to the station?
> Yes. Run!

2   These are . . . . cakes we've had for years, madam.
> Well, I'd prefer some that you've ordered more recently, please.

3   A hotel manager was talking to a new porter.
> Please call our guests by their names.
. . . . way to find out their names is to read the names on their suitcases.
The porter took his first guest to his room and said:
> I hope you enjoy your stay, Mr Real Leather.

"Thanks for the tip, Mr Leather."

4   What is . . . . answer to a teacher's questions in school?
> I don't know, sir.
Correct.

5   What was . . . . island in the world before Australia was discovered?
> I don't know. What was it?
Australia, of course.

6   Smith, what do we call . . . . ant in the world?
> An infANT, sir?

7   A man walked into a theatre looking for a job.
> What can you do? asked the theatre owner.
I can saw a woman in half.
> But that's . . . . trick in the business. Every magician I know can do it.
I know, said the man. But I do it lengthways!

8   What's . . . . place in the house to go to when you are dying?
> The living-room.

9   Jones, what is . . . . night of the year?
> A fortnight, sir?

10 I've got an easy job for . . . . person in the office. Who wants to do it?
Everybody put their hand up except one man.
> Why didn't you put your hand up? asked the boss.
I just couldn't be bothered! said the man.

I think the best way to learn English is to go to an English-speaking country. The word *way* is often used with the superlative. Can you complete these opinions:
I think the best way to make a lot of money is to ...
I feel the best way to help poor countries is to ...
I think the best way to meet new friends is to ...
The best way to keep fit is to ...

59 Comparison with *like*

Complete these jokes by putting one of the following words or expressions in the gaps provided:

a pullover   *the letter 'T'*   *a hawk*   *a cup of tea*   *stars*
a new man   *an idiot*   *lightning*   *one of the family*   *a glove*

1   Do you feel like . . . .?
    > Why? Do I look like one?

2   Why is an island like . . . .?
    > I don't know.
    Because it's always in the middle of water.

3   You are certainly hammering these nails in like . . . .
    > You mean that I'm very fast?
    No, you never strike in the same place twice!

4   Hello, Malcolm. How are you enjoying married life?
    > After my honeymoon I feel like . . . .
    And how does your wife feel?
    > Oh, she said she feels the same!

5   Why is a teacher like a bird of prey?
    > Because he watches you like

    . . . .

6   A new teacher went into her class of
    students for the first time. One student was
    jumping on top of his desk and making
    animal noises.
    > Stop acting like . . . ., the teacher shouted.
    He's not acting, said the student at the next desk.

7   Why are false teeth like . . . .?
    > I don't know.
    Because they always come out at night.

8   Our dog is like . . . .
    > Which one?

9   An eager sales assistant was trying his best to sell a woman a coat which was too small
    for her.
    > Well, madam. The coat fits you like . . . .
    The woman looked at herself in the mirror and said:
    > Yes, it's a pity it doesn't fit me like a coat!

10 Why is a banana skin like . . . .?
    > I've no idea.
    Because it's so easy to slip on!

What names of animals complete these comparisons?
    He fought like a ...   He walks like a ...He ate like a ...   He drinks like a ...
Are they the same in your language?

Section Eight

Clauses

Relative clauses

The main problem in this section is the difference between defining and non-defining relative clauses. This is not an area to spend too much time on. They mostly present a punctuation problem in written English. It is worth mentioning that many native speakers find them problematical.

Non-defining relative clauses

Most relative clauses are of this kind – where the clause merely adds an extra piece of information:

He introduced me to his sister, *who is retired and lives in America.*
(The sister just happens to be retired and living in America.)

My boss, *who's Irish*, is on holiday this week.
(My boss just happens to be Irish.)

In both these examples, we use commas to show that it is an extra piece of information.

Defining relative clauses

These clauses add an extra piece of information which helps to define the noun more clearly. Notice there are no commas to show the close link between the clause and its subject.

He introduced me to his sister *who is retired and lives in America.*
(He has more than one sister. This one is retired and lives in America.)

The person *who deals with your account* is on holiday this week.
(Several people work in the Accounts Department. One of them is on holiday at the moment. She deals with your account.)

Underline the defining relative clauses in the following jokes. The first is done for you.

1   I know a man <u>who married his sister</u>.
> But that's against the law!
Not if you're a priest, it isn't!

2   In a court of law the people in the public gallery were becoming very noisy. To make himself heard, the judge shouted:
> The next person who interrupts this trial will be thrown out of this court.
Hooray! shouted the prisoner.

3   A man walked into a police station and said:
> I've come about the job that's advertised outside.
What job? asked the policeman.
> The one on the poster outside that says: MAN WANTED FOR BURGLARY.

4   A man was run over by a car. A policeman asked:
> Did you see the person who was driving the car?
Not really, said the man. But I know it was my wife.
> But how do you know it was your wife if you didn't see the person who was driving the car?
Because I'd recognise her laugh anywhere!

5   Is there a word in the English language which contains all the vowels?
> Unquestionably!

6   A man with very long hair was getting his hair cut.
> Are you the person who cut my hair last time I was here? he asked the hairdresser.
I don't think so, the hairdresser replied. I've only been working here for a year.

7   What do you call a large brown animal that has flat feet, a large hump, and is found in Alaska?
> I don't know.
A lost camel!

8   Did you hear about the man who put his false teeth in backwards?
> No. What happened?
He ate himself!

9   Doctor, the pills that you gave me for my headache aren't doing me any good at all.
> Why not? They've worked well with other patients.
Because I can't get the top off the bottle!

10   What do you call a man who can't stop buying small carpets?
> I've no idea. What DO you call a man who can't stop buying small carpets?
A rug addict!

People who talk in the cinema really annoy me. We are all annoyed by the behaviour of others at times. **What or who annoys you?**

People who ...   *Cars drivers who ...*   *Teachers who ...*
TV programmes that ... *Politicians who ...*   *Friends who*

61 Non-defining Relative Clauses

Underline the non-defining relative clauses in the following jokes. The first one is done for you.

1   Little Lawrence, <u>who was a noisy, spoilt child,</u> was running up and down the aisle of an aeroplane. One annoyed passenger stopped him and said:
> Listen, kid. Why don't you go outside and play for a while!

2   A scientist was addressing a conference.
> Gentlemen, he announced proudly. I have created an incredible new acid. This acid, which I think is the answer to the problem of waste disposal, eats up and gets rid of everything that is put into it.
The scientist stood proudly, awaiting a response. A voice from the back of the auditorium broke the silence:
> And what kind of container do you keep this amazing acid in?

3   Harold went up to a man at a party, who he thought he recognised, and said:
> It's good to see you again after all these years. But how you've changed! Your hair is different; you've lost weight; you're a little shorter and you've stopped wearing glasses. What happened to you, Mr Frost?
But I'm not Mr Frost!
> Amazing! You've even changed your name!

4   Farmer Jack's special chicken, which lays square eggs, cost him nearly £1000.
> That's an expensive chicken. Can it talk as well?
Sure, but it only says one thing.
> And what's that?
Ouch!

5   Two prisoners escaped from Wandstreet Prison today. Sky-high Stevens, the train robber, who is 3 metres tall, and Mad Mitch, the Midget Murderer, who is only one metre tall, climbed over the prison wall in the early hours of the morning. Police are hunting high and low for them!

6   Two children were watching a speedboat, which was pulling a man on water skis across a lake.
> What makes the boat go so fast? asked one child.
I think it's because the man on the string is chasing it, said the other.

7   Dr Savage was angry when he sat down at an official dinner party. He had spent thirty minutes giving advice on a personal health problem to a complete stranger.
> Do you think I should send him a bill? he asked a solicitor, who was sitting next to him.
Why not? the solicitor replied. You provided a professional service to him.
> Thanks, the doctor said, I think I'll do that.
When the doctor went to his surgery next day to send the bill to the man, he found a letter from the solicitor which read: For legal services provided, £100.

A non-defining relative clause adds extra information:
My sister, <u>who lives in Canada,</u> is coming to visit us next month.
A defining relative clause helps to define more clearly the noun it follows:
My sister <u>who lives in Canada</u> is going to visit my sister <u>who lives in California.</u>

How would you translate these two sentences into your own language?
Try to make two sentences which show the difference between these two types of clause.

62 Clauses with participles

Complete these jokes by using either the present participle (*making*) or past participle (*made*) of one of the following verbs:

make	*talk*	*hypnotise*	*wear*	*excite*
eat	*swim*	*lie*	*live*	*play*

1   Yesterday I met a man . . . . sunglasses in the rain.
> That's stupid!
Not so stupid. He said they protect his eyes from all the umbrellas.

2   This is our most popular coat, madam, ... from the finest marino wool.
> Can I wear it in wet weather?
Of course, madam. Have you ever seen a sheep with an umbrella?

3   The local priest said, "Good Morning" to Mrs Watson and her young son in the street,
> Who was that man? asked her son.
Oh. That's the man who married me.
Her little son thought for a moment, then said:
> Well, who is the man . . . . in our house that I call "daddy"?

4   Mum, can I go into the sea?
> No.
Why not?
> Because the sharks . . . .
in these waters are dangerous.
But dad is already in there.
> Yes, darling. But he's insured!

"Don't worry darling.
Daddy's insured."

5   David and Tommy were sitting in a pub
. . . . about animals.
> I've just bought a pig, said David.
But where will you keep it? You haven't got a garden.
> I'm going to keep it under my bed.
But what about the smell?
> Oh! The pig will soon get used to that!

6   Stephan was a brilliant violinist. He believed that he could tame wild animals with his music, so he walked into the jungle, ... his violin. After a few minutes, elephants, giraffes, lions and monkeys stood around, ... by the music. Then a crocodile came out of the river, walked up to the violinist and ate him. All the other animals shouted, "Why on earth did you do that?" The crocodile simply said, "Eh?"

7   Little Alice was visiting her grandmother. She was playing alone in the living-room where there was a large cat . . . . by the fire. After a few minutes the cat woke up and saw Alice. It started to purr loudly. Alice looked at the cat in panic and rushed into the kitchen and shouted to her grandmother, "Come quick. The cat's started to boil!"

8   A man was standing at a bus stop . . . . fish and chips. An old lady and her little white dog stood next to him. The dog, ... by the smell of the fish and chips, started to bark and jump up on the man's leg.
> Do you mind if I throw him a bit? the man said to the old lady.
Not at all, she said. Go ahead.
So the man picked up the little dog and threw it over a wall.

Can you translate these sentences into your own language:
He was standing at the corner, *waiting for a taxi.*
I left university, *wishing I had worked a lot harder.*

63   Noun Clauses

Complete the jokes by using one of the following noun clauses:

you buried your grandmother yesterday
the cat ate your dinner
you've taken an interest in the goldfish
Dr Frankenstein has crossed an ostrich with a centipede

anything you ask for
you can't swim yet
your son needs glasses
I'm still living

1   You are the manager of this rock group, aren't you?
    > That's right. What can I do for you?
    Does the band take requests?
    > Yes. I'm sure that they'll be able to play . . . .
    Wonderful! Could you ask them to play cards, and stop making that horrible noise!

2   First scientist: Are you aware that . . . . ?
    Second scientist: What did he get?
    First scientist: We don't know. We haven't managed to catch it yet.

3   I understand that . . . .
    > Yes. I'm afraid we had to. She was dead!

4   Anne, I'm disappointed that . . . . You've been to the pool
    hundreds of times and spent hours in the water!
    > But, sir, replied Anne, I've been breathing air every day of my life and I still can't fly!

5   Mrs Templeton, are you absolutely certain that . . . . ?
    > Not really. They were his father's and I didn't want to throw them out.

6   Mrs Baker was a terrible cook. One night her husband came
    home from work and there was nothing on the table.
    > What's for dinner tonight? he asked.
    I'm afraid that . . . .,
    his wife replied.
    > Oh well, said Mr Smith sarcastically,
    I suppose I'll have to buy another cat!

7   Well, Bobby, I'm pleased that
    . . . .
    Have you been feeding them regularly?
    > Yes, Dad.
    And have you given them fresh water?
    > What do you mean? They haven't finished the water I gave them last month!

8   Doctor, it's a wonder that . . . . I have a pain in my head. I can't
    stop coughing. I've lost a lot of weight. I can't move my left arm and . . .
    Ten minutes later the patient was still listing his problems. The doctor started to write
    something down.
    > Are you writing me a prescription?
    No, it's a letter of introduction to the local undertaker!

Can you finish the following in ways that are true for you:
    I'm a bit disappointed that ...
    I'm pleased that ...

    I'm absolutely certain that ...
    I'm not very happy that ...

64   So / because

Complete these jokes using *so* or *because*:

1   Why does a young lady need the letter Y?
> I don't know. Tell me why.
> . . . . without it, she would be a young lad!

2   A tourist was walking in the mountains with a guide. He looked over a very steep cliff.
> That looks really dangerous. There really should be a sign here warning of the danger.
We had a warning sign up here for ten years, said the guide, but nobody fell over the side
. . . . we took it down.

3   I think it's true that television causes violence.
> Why do you say that?
. . . . every time I put the television on, my father hits me.

4   Why did so many students go to the headmaster's funeral?
> . . . . they could be sure he was really dead!

5   Excuse me, but why do you have two fried eggs on your head?
> . . . . boiled eggs would roll off, stupid!

6   Why can people never starve in the desert?
> . . . . of the sand which is always there!

7   I've got 100 goldfish.
> Where do you keep them?
In the bath.
> But what do you do when you want to have a bath?
Oh, I blindfold the fish . . . . they can't see me!

8   My Auntie June is very mean.
> Why do you say that?
. . . . she puts a fork in the sugar bowl when we visit her!

9   My husband had two interests in life: books and reading. Last week I gave him five
different books about the dangers of smoking . . . . he has decided to give up
reading!

10   I used to be a tap dancer.
> Really!
Yes, but I kept falling into the sink and breaking my leg . . . . I had to stop.

11   Why are cooks among the cruellest people on earth?
> . . . . they are always beating and whipping things!

12   Why do giraffes have such long necks?
> I don't know. Tell me why giraffes have such long necks.
. . . . that they can't smell their feet!

I couldn't be a good basketball player because of my height. Write some sentences about
yourself using the pattern: *I couldn't ... because ... .*

65 So + adjective + that

Complete the jokes by putting the words in the brackets in the correct order:

1 My grandfather was very fat.
> How fat was he?
Well, he was so fat that when he had a shower *(stayed feet and his dry legs)*
. . . .

2 My dad is so old that his hair is turning grey!
> That's nothing. My dad's so old that *(grey is his wig turning)*
. . . .

3 There's a road intersection in the centre of Paris that is so big and busy that they had to
(traffic hire an direct octopus to) . . . .

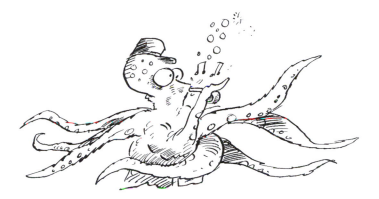

4 How tall are the giant redwood trees in the USA?
> Well, the trees are so tall that squirrels have to wear *(collect masks to nuts oxygen)*
. . . .

5 The hotel was terrible. It was so damp that the paper was coming off the wall.
> That's nothing. I once stayed in a hotel which was so damp that *(mousetraps they fish in their caught)* . . . . !

6 Harry is so thirsty that *(out is his hanging tongue)* . . . .
> Oh! I thought it was his tie.

7 I believe some of the world's most beautiful women come to this beach.
> Yes, they are so attractive that even *(the out tide to refuses go)*
. . . . when they are here.

8 Did you eat much at that new French restaurant?
> No. It was so expensive that I took one look at *(my lost and menu the appetite)*
. . . .

9 I hear they have very big oysters in Fiji.
> Yes. They are so large that the natives use the pearls they find inside them *(tenpin play to bowling)* . . . .

10 How old is your grandmother?
> I don't know exactly. She is so old that when I tried to count the candles on her cake at her birthday party, *(back me drove heat the)* . . . .

I'm so hungry that I could eat a horse! Use your imagination and write some sentences about yourself with the pattern: *I'm so ... that ... .*

66   Such + adjective + noun

Complete the jokes by putting one of the following nouns in the gaps provided:

temperatures	*feet*	*eyes*	*detective*	*ears*
town	*mouth*	*walls*	*woman*	*young man*

1   Is it true that Mary's new boyfriend is not very good-looking?
    > I'm afraid so. He has such big . . . . that he looks like a taxi with both doors open.

2   How's your new flat?
    > Terrible! It has such thin . . . . that I got six different answers to a question I asked my wife last night.

3   My uncle works for the fire service in Australia.
    > What does he do?
    He has such enormous . . . . that the fire service use him to stamp out forest fires.

4   I hear that Mrs Wilson finds it difficult to control her emotions.
    > Yes. She's such an emotional . . . . that she even cries when the traffic lights are against her.

5   Do you think PC Smith should join the CID and help in criminal investigations?
    > No. He's such a useless . . . . that he would have trouble following an elephant with a bleeding trunk in the snow.

6   Our teacher says we give him insomnia.
    > Does he look tired?
    Definitely! He has such bloodshot . . . .
    that they look like maps of the London
    Underground.

7   My son has great difficulty taking his medicine.
    > Is it because he doesn't like it?
    No. He has such a small . . . . that we
    have to use a shoe horn to give him an aspirin.

8   You say that Healthsville is the healthiest place in America. What age do people usually live to?
    > Well, it's impossible to say at the moment. It's such a healthy . . . . that the only man who has died so far is the undertaker.
    What did he die of?
    > Starvation!

9   The summer has been very hot this year.
    > It sure has. My father is a chicken farmer and it's causing him problems. There have been such high . . . . recently that he has had to feed his chickens ice to stop them laying hard-boiled eggs!

10 Harry is such a shy . . . . that he goes to the bathroom and locks the door when he wants to change his mind.

Can you think of ways of finishing these sentences?
It's been <u>such a long time</u> since I ... that ...
It's <u>such a long way</u> to ... that ...
I've got <u>such a lot of work</u> to do that I ...
We're <u>such good friends</u> that ...

Section Nine
Questions
and
Reported Speech

Rules for Reported Speech

Beware of being too dogmatic about this area. Some grammars say that certain rules must be followed, but the truth is that many different combinations of tenses are possible:

He said > he's coming / he'll come / he's going to come / he was coming.

On the whole, past tenses are used to report past events. Sometimes we report in the present things which are happening or are going to happen. From a classroom point of view it means we need to be very careful about giving rules.

Some exercises in the past asked students to turn direct speech into indirect speech. For example:

1. "What are you doing?"
   > *He asked me what I was doing.*

2. "I'm not doing that. It's too risky!"
   > *He refused to do it.*

It is very unnatural to report what someone has said verbatim as in example 1. We usually report the whole event in our own words as in example 2.

Tags

When teaching tags, the temptation is to concentrate on getting the correct auxiliary. Two other points are worth remembering:

1. Why tags are used in conversation – to facilitate turn-taking.

2. Tags are not questions – they need a response, which will give more information to enable the conversation to develop further:

You've been to Malta before, haven't you?
> Yes, but it was years ago.
Really, when was that?

67 Reported Speech

Complete the jokes below by putting *asked, said* or *told* in the gaps provided:

1 A man went into a hotel and saw a large dog sitting next to the reception desk.
> Does your dog bite? he asked the receptionist.
No, she said. So the man bent down to stroke the dog. It jumped up and bit his hand.
> I thought you . . . . that your dog didn't bite.
The receptionist got up from her seat and looked over her desk at the dog and replied:
> That's not my dog!

2 Mum, today the teacher . . . . me if I had any brothers or sisters.
> That's nice of her to take an interest in you. What did she say when you . . . . her you were an only child?
She said, "Thank goodness."

3 A young and very beautiful woman was talking to an old school friend.
> My husband tricked me into marrying him. Before we married he . . . . me that he was a multi-millionaire.
But he is a multi-millionaire, isn't he?
> Yes. But he also . . . . he was eighty-one and in very poor health and I've just found out that he is only seventy and he's in perfect condition.

4 A young lady went into a bank to cash a large cheque. The cashier . . . . her to identify herself so she took a mirror from her bag and looked into it.
> Yes, that's me all right, she said.

5 Waiter, what are these coins doing in my soup?
> Well, sir, you . . . . you would stop coming to this restaurant unless there was some change in the meals.

6 Sam . . . . me last night if I liked his company.
> What did you say?
I . . . . I didn't know which company he worked for.

7 Every time a visitor came to Mary Anderson's house her six-year-old son kicked the visitor on the leg and held on to it. One day she took him to a child psychologist. The child immediately kicked him on the leg. Calmly, the psychologist bent down and said something to the child. The child let go of the psychologist's leg immediately and ran to his mother. "Wonderful. He's cured!" Mary cried in delight. "What did you say to him?"
"I . . . . him that I'd smash his face in if he didn't let my leg go!"

"I'll smash your face in!"

8 She . . . . that she'd like her children young.
> But who would want old children?

When I was at school we were told not to write on the desks, not to smoke, and not to run in the corridors.
What were you told not to do when you were at school?

68 Do you know / Can you tell

Complete these jokes by putting the direct questions in brackets in the correct form:

1   Jones! Can you tell the class . . . . ? *(how do you spell elephant)*
    > E-L-E-F-A-N-T, sir.
    The dictionary spells it E-L-E-P-H-A-N-T.
    > But, sir, you didn't ask me how the dictionary spelt it!

2   A girl was standing in the middle of a busy road. A concerned man went up to her and said:
    > Is everything all right?
    Yes, said the young girl. Can you tell me . . . . ?
    (how can I get to the local hospital)
    > The man looked at the girl in the middle of the road.
    Yes. Just stay right where you are! he said.

3   Do you know . . . . ? *(what do vegetarian cannibals eat)*
    > No. What could they possibly eat?
    Swedes!

4   Do you know . . . . *(what's the time)* if your clock strikes 13?
    > Time to get a new clock!

5   Do you know . . . . ? *(where is your mother)*
    > She's round at the front.
    I know what she looks like, I want to know where she is!

6   An American tourist walked out of his hotel in the middle of the Sahara Desert. He was wearing nothing but his swimming trunks and carrying his beach towel. A local man came along on his camel and the American said:
    > Can you tell me . . . . ?
    (where is the sea)
    It's nearly 100 kilometres from here, said the Arab.
    > Now, this is what I call a beach, said the American.

"Now, this is what I call a beach!"

7   A chemistry teacher was testing his students.
    > Now. Does anybody know . . . .
    . . . . ?
    (what is the chemical formula for water)
    H-I-J-K-L-M-N-O, sir.
    > What do you mean?
    Well, my dad said it was H to O.

8   Smith, can you tell me . . . . ? *(what kind of insect is a slug)*
    > Er . . . a snail with a housing problem, sir?

I'd like to know why the British eat so many potatoes!
Can you tell me why the British drive on the left?
Work with a partner asking each other things you want to know about the British or the Americans. Start with *I'd like to know ...* or *Can you tell me why ... .*

Complete these jokes with a suitable question tag:

1 Collins, you did say you wanted yesterday off work because you were seeing your dentist, ... ?
> That's right, sir.
But didn't I see you coming out of the cinema in the afternoon with a friend?
> That was my dentist, sir!

2 Madam, you've put too many stamps on this letter.
> Oh dear, it won't go further than I want it to, ... ?

3 A car knocked a pedestrian down.
> What's the matter with you? shouted the pedestrian. Are you blind?
What do you mean – blind? said the driver. I hit you, ... ?

4 I don't want a car. I need a cow, said the farmer.
> You can't ride a cow through the town centre, ... ? said the salesman.
True. But I can't milk a new car, ... ?
replied the farmer.

5 Maria, you're an identical twin, ... ?
> Yes.
How does your mother tell you apart?
> That's easy. My brother has a moustache.

6 My doctor says I can't play tennis.
> Oh, so he has played with you too, ... ?

7 Doctor, come quickly.
> What's the problem?
We can't get into our house.
> It's not really a job for a doctor, ... ?
I think it is. My baby has swallowed the front door key.

8 Why do people always put the right shoe on first?
> I don't know.
Well, it would be silly to put the wrong shoe on, ... ?

9 I've never flown before, said the nervous lady to the pilot. You will bring me down safely, ... ?
> All I can say, madam, is that I've never left anybody up there yet.

10 Mary told her father that she and her boyfriend, Harry, wanted to get married.
> So, said Mary's father. You want to become my son-in-law, ... ?
Not really, but I don't have much choice, ... ?

Can you translate into your own language the following sentences so that there is a clear difference in meaning:

You're going out with Jane tonight, aren't you?
You're not going out with Jane tonight, are you?
You're going out with Jane tonight, are you!

70   So / neither / either

Complete these jokes by putting *so*, *neither*, or *either* in the gaps provided:

1   Why don't you play chess with Gregor any more?
> Would you play with somebody who cheats?
No, I wouldn't.
> Well, ... would Gregor.

2   I can't believe that John is in hospital. Only yesterday he was the picture of good health.
I saw him with a beautiful young blonde girl in a French restaurant.
> . . . . did his wife!

3   I was in Switzerland on a business trip last week.
> . . . . was I.
I didn't see much of the scenery though.
> . . . . did I. There were too many mountains in the way!

4   Waiter, this food is terrible. Get the manager!
> There's no point. He won't eat it . . . . , sir.

5   A politician was visiting a psychiatric hospital.
A smartly dressed man came up to him and said:
> I flew to France last week.
. . . . did I, said the politician.
> And how do you feel now? asked the man.
What do you mean? replied the politician.
> Well, aren't your arms tired?

6   I've borrowed my neighbour's bagpipes.
> But you can't play the bagpipes!
I know, but . . . . can my neighbour, if I have them!

7   A cow wanted to cross a river to reach the green grass on the other side. There were no
bridges and the river was fast and deep. How did the cow get across?
> I give up.
. . . . did the cow!

8   I eat in a different restaurant every night!
> I don't give tips . . . .

9   A very rich and extremely fat lady walked into a very expensive London store. In a loud
voice she called to the manager:
> I would like to see a dress that fits me.
. . . . would I, the manager said quietly to himself.

10   Doctors say that whisky can't cure the common cold.
> Yes, but . . . . can doctors!

Most people think that taking drugs is crazy, and so do I.
Give some of your views on the following topics with this structure (*Most people think ... and
so ... I*):

your school days   *young people today*   *the Government*
the United Nations   *terrorists*   *satellite television*
income tax   *morality today*   *the sixties*

71   What's your name?

Complete these jokes with the following words or phrases:

she has a heart of stone   *My name is White*   *Piggy*   *He can't talk yet*
What's your name?   *It's Sweetheart*   *Sir Harold*   *I think it's Sitboy*

1   My mother had a baby last night.
    > That's wonderful. Is it a boy or a girl?
    A boy.
    > And what's your new brother's name?
    I don't know. . . . .

2   A rich boy was at his new school for the first time. He said to the boy sitting next to him:
    > I keep all my money in the Bank of England. What's the name of your bank?
    The boy thought for a moment, then said: . . . .

3   A postman was having trouble delivering his letters because it was raining hard and some
    were getting wet. It was difficult to read some of the names and addresses clearly. He
    called at one house and said to the owner:
    > What's your name, sir? The name on this letter is smudged.
    Sorry, the man replied. . . . .

4   Two dogs met in a park.
    > My name's Rover, said the first dog. What's your name?
    I'm not sure, replied the second dog. But . . . .

5   What's your name, boy?
    > Harold.
    Say 'sir' when you speak to me. Now boy,
    what's your name?
    > . . . .

6   What do you call your girlfriend?
    > Sun.
    Why Sun?
    > Because she's always so bright and happy.
    I call my girlfriend Peach.
    > Is that because she's soft and sweet?
    No. I call her Peach because

    . . . .

"Sit boy?"

7   In a very crowded supermarket a young man pushed a woman accidentally. Before he
    had time to apologise, the woman glared at him and shouted angrily:
    > Excuse me, young man. But who do you think you are pushing?
    I've no idea, replied the young man. . . . .

8   Wilfred Potts was the director of a large company. He was talking to his new chauffeur.
    > What's your name, driver?
    Nigel, sir.
    > I always call my employees by their surname. What's your surname, driver?
    . . . ., sir.
    Mr Potts was silent for a few moments, then said:
    > Drive on, Nigel.

What's she called? What's her first name? What's her surname? Does she have a middle name?
Work with a partner. Ask about each other's relations.

Section Ten
Prepositions

The correct preposition

Sometimes there is a situation where only one preposition is 'correct'. For example:

> We arrived *at* 8 o'clock.

Very often, more than one preposition is possible depending on the meaning. All the following correct examples have subtly different meanings:

I'll meet you *at* the station.	I'll meet you *beside* the station.
I'll meet you *in* the station.	I'll meet you *behind* the station.
I'll meet you *by* the station.	I'll meet you *inside* the station.
I'll meet you *in front of* the station.	I'll meet you *around* the station.

Expressions with prepositions

Most prepositions have a literal meaning which we are all familiar with: *on, in, at, through, etc.* When prepositions are part of an expression, it is important to learn the whole expression. There is usually no point in trying to explain why a particular preposition is used. For example:

a cheque *for £200*	go *on strike*
a good memory *for faces*	pay *in advance*

The best advice is to teach expressions like these as 'wholes'.

Phrasal verbs

Phrasal Verbs are among the commonest examples of expressions with prepositions. It is perhaps better to refer to such 'prepositions' as 'particles' so that students see a clear difference between the prepositional use and their use as 'part' of the phrasal verb. *It took me ages to get through to John* has got some idea of the literal meaning of *through*, but *I don't get on with him* has no idea of *on* combined with *with*. These very important verbs simply have to be learned as if each was a whole expression. The particle cannot be divorced from the verb.

72   Prepositions of Place

Complete these jokes by putting a suitable preposition of place in the gaps provided:

1   Waiter, there's a fly . . . . my soup.
    > Don't worry, sir. The spider . . . . your bread will eat it.

2   Haven't I seen your face somewhere else?
    > No, I don't think so. My face has always been . . . . my ears.

3   Crime in New York is very bad. Last week a man said to me:
    > Do you want to buy a watch?
    Let me see it first, I asked.
    > Keep your voice down, he said. The man . . . . to you is still wearing it.

4   Well, son, how are your marks from school?
    > They're . . . . water.
    What do you mean?
    > They're . . . . C level.

5   Bobby, if you found £2 . . . . one pocket and £5 . . . . the other one, what
    would you have?
    > The wrong trousers, sir!

6   Is it raining . . . . ?
    > What a silly question!
    Why?
    > Well, does it ever rain . . . . ?

7   What would you do if an elephant sat
    . . . . you in the cinema?
    > I would miss most of the film.

8   My dog is a nuisance. He chases everyone
    . . . . a bicycle. What can I do?
    > Take his bicycle away.

9   How did you cut your nose?
    > Do you see that door . . . . there?
    Yes, I see it.
    > Well, I didn't.

10 Dad, there's a black cat . . . . the kitchen table.
    > That's OK, son. Black cats are lucky.
    Well, this one certainly is. It's eating your dinner!

11 When an elephant sits . . . . your chair, what time is it?
    > Time to get a new chair!

12 How do you get an elephant . . . . a telephone box?
    > Open the door!

My car once broke down <u>on</u> the way <u>back from</u> holiday.
We used to live <u>in</u> an old cottage <u>in</u> a small village <u>in</u> the country <u>on</u> the edge of a forest.
Can you make up sentences with as many prepositions of place as possible?

73   Prepositions of Direction

Complete these jokes by putting a suitable preposition of direction in the gaps provided:

under	over	down	round	through
up on	up	out of	along	away from

1   I knew you needed glasses before you said a word, sir, said the optician.
> How did you know that?
When you walked . . . . the window.

2   Waiter! Do you have frogs' legs?
> Yes, sir.
Well, jump . . . . the bar and get me a beer!

3   How did you get that nasty cut on your forehead?
> I bit myself.
How on earth did you manage that?
> I climbed . . . . a chair!

4   A young boy and an old man were standing on a bus. As more passengers tried to get on the driver shouted:
> Move farther . . . . the bus.
He's not my father, replied the boy. He's my grandad!

5   The police stopped an old lady for driving too fast.
> Madam. As you drove . . . . the corner,
we both thought, "Eighty", at least.
Oh no, officer. You're wrong. I've just turned sixty.

6   Graham's mother told him to get . . . . the house and do something.
> But what will I do? asked Graham.
Go window shopping, suggested his mother.
> Two hours later Graham came home with five windows.

7   Henry met his mother as he was climbing . . . . a hill.
> Where are you going? she asked.
I'm going to watch the sun rise. Henry replied.
> All right dear, but don't get too close.

8   I once came face to face with a lion.
> Really! What happened?
Well, I didn't have a gun, and the lion growled and came closer and closer.
> What did you do?
I moved . . . . to the next cage!

9   Mr Brown, can you explain to the court why you pushed one of your friends . . . .
a steamroller?
> I needed a new flatmate, your honour!

10   The doctor told my sister to do some exercises every day to reduce her weight.
> So what's she doing?
She pushes herself . . . . the table about forty times a day!

How many of the following verbs collocate with *through*:
    fly   walk   go   speak   ride   work   live   get
Match them up with the following objects: *the twentieth century, the recession, money like water, the door, turbulence, an examination, an interpreter, a storm.*

Some nouns are followed by a particular preposition. Complete the jokes by putting a suitable preposition in the gaps provided:

1   We've just bought a new dog. Would you like to come round and play with it?
> Does it bite?
I'm not sure. That's the reason . . . . asking you to come over!

2   I'm beginning to doubt whether I have a loving relationship . . . . my parents.
> Why do you say that?
When I got home from school last week, they had moved house!

3   My wife and I had an argument . . . . where to go last night. She wanted to go to the ballet and I wanted to go to a rock concert. But we soon came to an agreement.
> And what was the ballet like?

4   Did you hear about the worker in a banana-packing firm?
> Oh, yes, he got the sack . . . .
throwing the bent ones away!

5   What was the cause . . . . the large bump on your head?
> My wife threw some tomatoes at me.
But how could tomatoes do such damage to your head?
> Easy. They were still in the tin!

6   Darling, do you have a good memory . . . . faces?
> Yes, I think so. Why do you ask?
Because I've just broken your shaving mirror!

7   How did you break your leg?
> It was the result . . . . following my doctor's prescription.
But how could you break your leg doing that?
> Well, the prescription blew out of the window and I followed it!

8   The disadvantage . . . . being the world's shortest person is that you are the last person to know when it's raining.

9   You've written a cheque . . . . £200.
> Yes. I'm sending it to my sister for her birthday.
But you haven't signed it.
> I know. It's a surprise and I don't want her to know who sent it!

10 I see Mrs Thompson has notified us of her change . . . . address.
> Yes, dear. She's lucky. It's years since I had a change of a dress!

Now revise the prepositions from above by completing these expressions:

a change . . . address	the disadvantage . . . living	the result . . . winning
the cause . . . the war	the reason . . . leaving	a good memory . . . faces
an argument . . . money	a relationship . . . a woman	a cheque . . . £100
get the sack . . . stealing		

Complete these jokes using *in, at, for* or *on*:

1 What's . . . . the television tonight?
> Same as usual.
What's that?
> The indoor aerial!

2 Jane was very much . . . . love with Marco. One night they were sitting together on the sofa listening to music.
> Marco, darling, Jane said. Whisper something soft and sweet in my ear.
Marco put his lips to Jane's ear and said:
> Chocolate cream cake!

3 Look at the speed! said one bird to another as Concorde whizzed overhead.
> You would fly as fast as that if your tail was . . . . fire!

4 I went to the doctor about my bad memory.
> And what did he do?
He made me pay . . . . advance!

5 A man went into a small restaurant . . . .
lunch. He wasn't very happy with the food
he was given so he called the waiter over.
> Waiter, is this chicken pie or beef pie?
Can't you tell the difference? asked the waiter.
> No! said the man.
Then does it matter?

6 In Texas, everything is big. Texans live in huge houses and drive massive cars. A Texan was . . . . holiday in Africa. He was visiting the famous Victoria Falls, the largest waterfalls in the world.
> I don't think you have anything like this in Texas, said the guide.
No, said the Texan. But we have plumbers who could fix it!

7 David had a broken leg and he had to walk with crutches. He met an old friend who said:
> What happened? Did you have an accident?
No. I was hit by a large bull and it was no accident. The bull did it . . . . purpose!

8 Is your mum . . . . home? said a salesman to a little boy who was playing outside.
> Yes, said the boy.
The salesman knocked on the door of the house but nobody answered.
> I thought your mother was in? he said to the boy.
She is, the boy said. We live in the house next door.

9 Nice to see you again. You haven't changed at all.
> I know. The laundry has been . . . . strike for six months.

10 A waiter gave the menu to a customer. While the customer was looking at the menu the waiter scratched his bottom.
> Have you got an itchy bottom? asked the customer.
No, said the waiter. I've only got what's . . . . the menu.

How many other phrases can you make with *in, at,* and *on*:
IN . . . .
AT . . . .
ON . . . .

76 Before / after / until

Complete these jokes using *before*, *after*, or *until*:

1   What two things can you never eat . . . . breakfast?
    > Lunch and dinner.

2   Mr Lennon was leaving his hotel. It was a good hotel but he was shocked at the price of his room. He thought it was much too expensive. As he was leaving the hotel, the manager asked:
    > Well, sir. Did you enjoy your stay with us?
    Yes, but I'm sorry to leave the hotel so soon . . . . buying it!

3   The biology teacher was talking about the importance of oxygen to life on earth.
    > Without oxygen, human life would not be possible. This important gas was discovered in 1773.
    But sir, said one student. What did people breathe . . . . oxygen was discovered?

4   A policeman stopped a motorist for speeding.
    > Why were you driving so fast? asked the policeman.
    Well, said the motorist, my brakes aren't working very well, and I want to get home . . . . I have an accident!

5   Mr Maxwell couldn't sleep . . . .
    his wife left him.
    > Why? Did he miss her?
    No, she took the bed with her!

6   Mum, can I play the piano?
    > You can't touch it . . . . you've
    washed your hands.
    But mum, I promise I'll only play the black keys!

7   Two eggs were in a pot of boiling water.
    > Gosh! one said. It's getting hot in here.
    The heat's not the only problem, said the other.
    > What do you mean?
    Well, ... you leave here, you get your head bashed in!

8   Alison was sitting at her desk writing a letter.
    > Who are you writing to? asked her little sister.
    Myself.
    > What does the letter say?
    How do I know? I won't get it . . . . tomorrow!

9   Two little boys walked into a gallery of modern art by mistake. They stood in the middle of a large room and looked at all the modern paintings on the walls.
    > Quick, said one of the boys. Let's get out of here . . . . they blame this on us!

10 How does an elephant get down from a tree?
    > I don't know.
    It sits on a leaf and waits . . . . autumn arrives.

Complete this sentence in as many ways as you can think of:
I don't think there will be peace in ... until ... .

77 For / during / while

Complete these jokes using *for, during,* or *while*:

1 Dr Findlay was passing one of his patients in the street.
> Good morning, Mrs Merton. I haven't seen you . . . . a long time.
I know, doctor. I've been ill!

2 Jack was talking about his six months on holiday in Norway.
> . . . . the dark winter nights, I only wore white clothes.
Why?
> So that cars would see me clearly.
Did it work?
> No. I got knocked down by a snow plough!

3 A very heavy rainstorm started . . . . Stanley was visiting his friend, Robert.
Looking out of the window, Robert said to Stanley:
> You must stay the night with us. I insist!
Thanks very much, said Stanley. I'll just run home and get my pyjamas.

4 Herbert was very mean. One day a robber stopped him in an empty street and shouted:
> Your money or your life!
. . . . three minutes Herbert stood and looked intently at his feet.
> Come on! screamed the robber. Your money or your life. Which is it to be?
Quiet, said Herbert. I'm still thinking.

5 . . . . a hunting trip to Africa, an English explorer and his guide met a large leopard. The leopard started to run towards them. The guide began to panic and shouted to the Englishman, who had a gun:
> Quick. Shoot the leopard on the spot.
Be specific, said the explorer calmly. Which spot?

6 I lived on water . . . . six months.
> Really! When was that?
. . . . I was a sailor in the navy!

7 You think I'm fat, don't you, doctor?
> Why do you say that?
Well, ... my examination you said:
"Open your mouth, Mrs Penn, and say Mooooo!"

8 At school the teacher had introduced Charles to the theory of evolution. That evening, Charles decided to ask his mother about it . . . . they were having dinner.
> Mum, are we really descended from apes?
I don't know, replied his mother. I've never met your father's family!

9 . . . . the experiment we noticed that when we heat a piece of metal, it expands, and when we cool it, it contracts. Now can anybody give me another example of this?
> Well, sir. In summer the days are long and in winter they are short!

10 Why do you always part your hair in the middle?
> So that I will be evenly balanced . . . . I'm riding my bicycle!

I usually play a lot of tennis during the summer holidays.
Talk about yourself with this pattern: *I usually ... during the summer holidays.*

Complete the phrasal verbs in these jokes using the correct preposition:

1   What's the difference between a nail and a boxer?
> The first gets knocked . . . . and the second often gets knocked . . . . !

2   Doctor, I'm suffering from insomnia. I just sit and watch TV all night. What can I do?
> Do you watch TV sitting in a chair?
Yes.
> Can I suggest you change your position then? If you sit on the edge of the television, you'll find that you'll soon drop . . . . !

3   When is a car not a car?
> I don't know.
When it turns . . . . a garage!

4   Where's your dog?
> I had it put . . . .
Was it mad?
> Well, it wasn't exactly pleased about it.

5   A London restaurant claimed that it could supply any dish requested. A man decided to test the claim. He entered the restaurant and said:
> I'd like elephant ears on toast.
The waiter returned after a few seconds and said:
> I do apologise, sir, but we've run . . . . bread.

"Just dropping off!"

6   A man was on the point of being executed by firing squad.
> Would you like a last cigarette?
No, replied the man. I'm trying to give . . . . !

7   A poacher stole a duck from a lake. He pulled all its feathers off. He was about to kill the duck when the owner of the lake arrived, so he threw the duck into the water.
> You were trying to steal that duck, weren't you?
No.
> Well, how do you explain all the feathers around your feet?
Simple. The duck wanted to go for a swim so I'm looking . . . . its clothes.

8   At a party Arnold Powell was trying to impress one of the guests.
> My great-grandfather fought with Napoleon in Europe. My grandfather fought with the British. My father fought with the Australians. And I'm fighting with the Americans.
The guest looked at Arnold for a moment and said:
> Tell me something. Why can't your family get . . . . with anyone?

9   Mr Handel thought that his wife played the piano very well. One day he asked a famous music teacher to come to his house and listen to his wife.
> Do you think my wife should take . . . . the piano as a career? Mr Handel asked.
The music teacher thought her playing was terrible and said:
No, I think she should put the lid down as a favour.

**Have you ever *taken up* a sport or hobby? Do you *get on with* all your relations?
Have you ever *dropped off* in the middle of a class?**

Section Eleven
Other Points

Miscellaneous points

This final section contains 4 points which do not naturally fit in any of the others. The grammar of English is not a neat system. There are grey areas and areas which overlap. It is worth discussing this with students so that they do not have the idea that grammar is a simple matter of right and wrong. It is true that when we focus on grammar in class we are interested in accuracy, but it is worth pointing out that grammar allows us to express meaning. For example, the difference between the Present Simple and Continuous is a difference of meaning as well as form.

79 Numbers

Complete these jokes by putting one of the following phrases in the gaps provided:

A train driver's egg sandwich   *All of them*   *Are you in trouble*
Let's see what he does with that   *Sweets*   *should accidentally fall*
Let me see the cup of tea first   *fell inside*   *Dark, isn't it*

1   A man is about to be shot by firing squad. The officer in charge asks him:
    > Do you have one last request?
    Yes, I'd like permission to sing a song.
    > Certainly, go ahead.
    A million green bottles standing on a wall. A million
    green bottles standing on a wall, and if one green bottle
    . . . ., there'd be 999,999 green bottles
    standing on a wall. 999,999 green bottles standing on a
    wall. 999,999 green bottles standing on a wall, and if
    one green bottle . . . ., there'd be
    999,998 green bottles standing on a wall ...

2   Come in, boat number 61. Your time is up.
    > Boss. We only have 50 boats.
    Oh! My goodness! Boat number 19!
    . . . .?

3   Now class. Give me a number with two digits?
    > 49, somebody shouted out. The teacher wrote 94 on the blackboard.
    Give me another number. said the teacher.
    > 35, somebody shouted out. The teacher wrote 53 on the blackboard.
    Give me another number.
    > A boy at the back of the class shouted 88. Then he turned to his friend and said:
    Now . . . .!

4   My sister works in a sweet shop. She's 17 years old and she is 1.25 metres tall. What does
    she weigh?
    > How on earth do you expect me to know that? What does she weigh?
    . . . ., of course!

5   What's yellow, white and brown and travels at 160 kilometres an hour?
    > I don't know.
    . . . .!

6   Jane. Which month of the year has twenty-eight days?
    . . . ., sir!

7   The Grand Hotel in my city has eighty-one floors. Yesterday my friend fell from a
    window on the top floor.
    > Oh dear! Is she dead?
    No, she . . . .!

8   Think of a number between one and twenty. Now double it. Multiply the total by four.
    Now subtract eighteen. Add three and take away the number you started with. Now close
    your eyes.
    > Yes.
    . . . .?

9   *(Man in street)*
    Excuse me, sir. Would you give me twenty pence for a cup of tea?
    I don't know. . . . .!

Write down, in words, numbers 98 to 102. Watch your spelling!

Complete these jokes by putting the words in brackets in the correct order:

1   How do you stop a cockerel crowing on a Sunday morning?
   > I don't know.
   . . . .! *(on night cook Saturday it)*

2   I'm sorry to disturb you at two o'clock in the morning, doctor.
   > Oh, that's all right. I had to . . . .!
   (up answer to telephone the get)

3   What great event happened in 1809?
   > Abraham Lincoln was born, sir.
   Correct. And what great event happened in 1812?
   > Er . . . Abraham Lincoln . . . .? *(third his had birthday)*

4   Why are soldiers always tired on the first of April?
   > I don't know.
   Because they have just. . . . .!
   (31 a days March finished of)

5   Why are you crying?
   > I hurt my finger, mum.
   When did you do that?
   > Thirty minutes ago.
   But I didn't hear you then.
   . . . .!
   (were I out you thought)

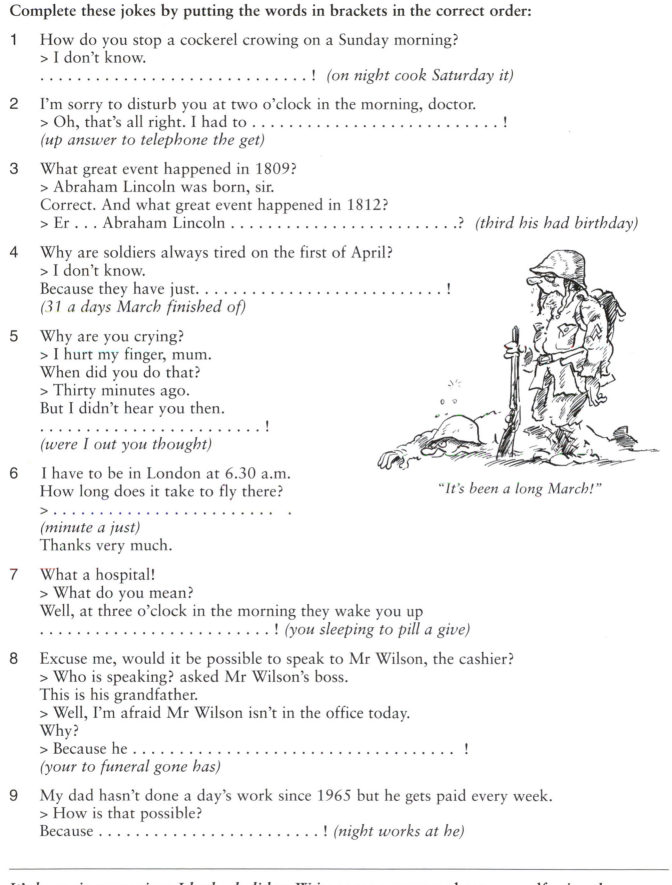

"*It's been a long March!*"

6   I have to be in London at 6.30 a.m.
   How long does it take to fly there?
   > . . . .
   (minute a just)
   Thanks very much.

7   What a hospital!
   > What do you mean?
   Well, at three o'clock in the morning they wake you up
   . . . .! *(you sleeping to pill a give)*

8   Excuse me, would it be possible to speak to Mr Wilson, the cashier?
   > Who is speaking? asked Mr Wilson's boss.
   This is his grandfather.
   > Well, I'm afraid Mr Wilson isn't in the office today.
   Why?
   > Because he . . . . !
   (your to funeral gone has)

9   My dad hasn't done a day's work since 1965 but he gets paid every week.
   > How is that possible?
   Because . . . .! *(night works at he)*

It's been six years since I had a holiday. **Write some sentences about yourself using the pattern:** *It's been ... (minutes, days etc) since I (past tense) ... .*
You could talk about your last holiday, your previous job, the last place you lived, where you studied, your last meal, your last meeting with a friend, etc.

81   Likes and Dislikes

Complete these jokes by putting one of the following phrases in the gaps provided:

my name's Martin
never cleaned one
apple tree is on fire
leave the holes on your plate
chocolate
Croaka Cola

the smell of its feet
prefer beef
especially at the cinema
have to play inside
the woman in the opposite flat

1   Dad, do you like baked apples?
> Yes. Why do you ask?
Because your . . . .

2   Dad, I hate cheese with holes in it.
> Well, just eat the cheese and . . . .!

3   What does love mean, Derek?
> Well, I like my mum and dad, but I love . . . .!

4   Why does a giraffe have such a long neck?
> Because it can't bear . . . .

5   Why do mother kangaroos hate rainy days?
> Because the children . . . .

6   Doctor, I think I've got flu.
> Well, put your head out of the window and stick your tongue out.
Will that make me better?
> No, but I can't stand . . . .

7   I adore men who are frank.
> Too bad, ...

8   What do frogs like to drink?
> . . . .

9   You can't like everybody, can you?
> You certainly can't. For example, I detest people who talk behind your back.
Yes, ...!

10 What's your favourite food?
> I'm very fond of spaghetti bolognese, sir.
Spell it.
> Actually, sir, I think I
. . . .

11 Do you like cleaning ladies?
I don't know. I've . . . .

I can't stand the sound of the dentist's drill. Write some sentences about yourself using the pattern: *I can't stand the (sound / sight / smell / taste) of ... .*

82 Requests with *would like*

Complete these jokes by putting one of the following words or phrases in the gaps provided:

full	*a new bike*	*married*	*pockets*	*die*
soon	*a return ticket*	*face*	*a submarine*	*coffee*

1   I'd like a room, please.
    > Single?
    . . . . , actually.

2   I'd like two tickets to the moon, please.
    > I'm sorry, sir, but the moon is . . . . at the moment.

3   Would you like to work on . . . . ?
    > No. I can't sleep without the windows open.

4   I'd like a mirror, please.
    > A hand mirror, madam?
    No, it's my . . . . I want to look at.

5   Would you like to buy a pocket calculator?
    > No thanks. I already know how many
    . . . . I have.

6   *(At the ticket office in a railway station)*
    I'd like . . . . , please.
    > Where to?
    Back here, of course.

7   Would you like some . . . . , sir?
    > Certainly.
    White or black?
    > White.
    Cream or milk?
    > Neither. Just a little pasteurised blend of water, corn syrup solids, vegetable oil, sodium caseinate, carrageenan, guargum, disodium phosphate, polysorbate 60, sorbitan monostearate and artificial colouring, please.

8   I'd like to know the exact place where I'll . . . .
    > But why?
    Because then I would never go there!

9   How would you like your steak, sir?
    > As . . . . as possible!

10 Son, what would you like for your birthday?
    > I've got my eye on . . . .
    Well, son. Keep your eye on it, because you'll never get your bottom on it!

I'd like to meet Carl Lewis because he is one of my heroes. Talk about who you would like to meet, and say why you'd like to meet them. Use the pattern: *I'd like to meet ... because ... .*

Answer Key

Unit 1

1. does, don't   2. Do   3. does, does, does, does   4. do, don't   5. does   6. do, do   7. Do, do   8. Does
9. doesn't   10. does, do

Unit 2

1. looking   2. flying   3. eating   4. chewing   5. telling   6. drowning   7. giving   8. waiting   9. trying
10. using

Unit 3

1. decided to leave   2. worked as a tax inspector   3. married the wrong man   4. smashed his false teeth
5. kissed her face   6. ended   7. didn't like her   8. always pulled

Unit 4

1. found   2. kept   3. sold, caught   4. saw, ran   5. fed, fed   6. broke, broke   7. threw   8. ate   9. shot
10. went, said, took, blew, gave

Unit 5

1. were, was, weren't   2. was, was, was   3. was, were, was   4. was, was   5. were   6. was, wasn't
7. were, were, was   8. was   9. were   10. were

Unit 6

1. was crawling, ate   2. was carrying, knocked, was looking   3. were you doing, fell, was passing, put
4. hit, sank, were lying, said   5. was giving, arrived   6. fell, was brushing   7. hit, was crossing, broke
8. smelled / smelt, was working

Unit 7

1. needed, performed   2. seen   3. had, shaved   4. caught   5. swum   6. worked   7. been   8. suffered
9. visited   10. come

Unit 8

1. have just bitten   2. have put   3. has swallowed   4. have just had   5. has been   6. have changed
7. have decided   8. have invented   9. have made   10. has stopped, has stopped

Unit 9

1. Have you ever been, found   2. sold, said, have failed, has fallen   3. have had, ate, Did they smell, took
4. has everyone read, did Lord Nelson die   5. bought, has just cheated   6. has gone, disappeared   7. has lost,
did she last see   8. has never visited, took, did your dad say   9. Have you caught, started

Unit 10

1. made it yet   2. in my pocket   3. for 93 years   4. ride a bike   5. not yet   6. just won't go away   7. all its
life   8. lost your voice

Unit 11

1. had   2. had   3. had, had, hadn't, had, had   4. had   5. had   6. hadn't   7. hadn't   8. had   9. had

Unit 12

1. following   2. walking   3. going   4. digging   5. standing   6. watching   7. playing   8. running

Unit 13

1. 'll   2. 'm going to   3. 'll   4. 'll   5. 'm going to   6. are you going to   7. 'll, 'll   8. 'm going to   9. are
going to   10. 'll

Unit 14

1. long   2. Emergency Exit   3. wet   4. looks   5. round   6. sober   7. fly   8. funeral   9. sleep   10. die

Unit 15

1. We're sending   2. you're moving   3. are you giving   4. are you coming, you go away   5. we're advertising
6. I begin   7. my daughter gets married, I'm losing, I am gaining   8. I'm growing, I'm growing   9. When
are you leaving?

Unit 16

1. leaving   2. entertaining   3. using / needing, needing / using   4. going   5. painting, keeping   6. asking
7. adopting   8. driving

Unit 17
1. used to be   2. used to saw   3. used to know   4. used to chase   5. used to dive   6. used to take   7. used to turn   8. used to be called   9. used to get, used to sit   10. used to study

Unit 18
1. Have   2. 've, 've, 've, 've, haven't   3. 've, 've   4. 's, hasn't   5. have, 've   6. 's   7. have   8. 've, have   9. has   10. hasn't

Unit 19
1. teeth   2. You love me   3. yes, no, yes, no   4. Which one   5. You're a taxi   6. bath   7. six cows   8. sore head   9. Jack, Queen, King   10. 4 to 6 years.

Unit 20
1. can, Can   2. can't   3. can't, can't, can't   4. can't   5. can't, can't   6. can, can't   7. can't   8. can   9. can't, could   10. couldn't

Unit 21
1. What size does your crocodile take   2. we don't make traps that big   3. you certainly can't take it with you   4. Phone all of them   5. Can his bike come out to play   6. No, you can't John   7. he didn't say anything   8. but look at the state the world is in   9. I'll go and have a look   10. That's what you gave me yesterday

Unit 22
1. look at it   2. stop her   3. the headmaster   4. fight for them   5. stop it   6. wake up until seven o'clock   7. spend it for you.   8. on the toilet door   9. go back tomorrow   10. have a door

Unit 23
1. mustn't   2. don't have to   3. mustn't   4. mustn't   5. don't have to   6. don't have to   7. don't have to   8. mustn't

Unit 24
1. must   2. must   3. must   4. must   5. must   6. can't   7. must   8. can't   9. must   10. must

Unit 25
1. should   2. Should   3. shouldn't, should, should   4. should, should   5. should   6. Should   7. shouldn't, should   8. shouldn't   9. should

Unit 26
1. should   2. should   3. should   4. shouldn't   5. should   6. shouldn't   7. shouldn't, should   8. should   9. should

Unit 27
1. you shout all the time   2. anything goes wrong   3. eat an apple every day for 1200 months   4. my husband doesn't like it   5. a teacher falls into the sea   6. you stand in front of the mirror   7. I'll give you one   8. it lands on its edge   9. you sit down   10. I give you £5.50 and £20.45

Unit 28
1. would   2. would, would, would, would   3. would   4. would   5. would, wouldn't, would, wouldn't   6. would   7. wouldn't   8. would   9. wouldn't   10. would

Unit 29
1. been   2. won   3. given   4. stolen   5. bought   6. stayed   7. taken   8. failed

Unit 30
1. that much money   2. tickets   3. your own coffee   4. the name   5. history   6. half an hour ago   7. car keys   8. will   9. will power   10. piano practice

Unit 31
1. Don't bite any   2. I'm drowning   3. Your daughter   4. you can't sleep in class   5. lose all my pigeons   6. kill yourself   7. my daughter's name   8. sew the hole in my shirt   9. in the window

Unit 32
1. was hit, was attacked, was robbed   2. was killed   3. am sent   4. am being served   5. were taken   6. are found   7. was invented   8. was stopped   9. was the tennis player given   10. was detained

Unit 33
1. has just been cut   2. Have your eyes ever been checked   3. has never been used   4. had been killed   5. have been asked   6. have already been scalped   7. have been missed   8. had been planted   9. had been shown, had been annoyed   10. had been chopped

Unit 34
1. hair   2. fingers   3. room   4. teeth   5. nails   6. head   7. Venetian blinds   8. the goal

Unit 35
1. forgot 2. promised, learning 3. refuse 4. want 5. need 6. trying 7. want, failed 8. hope 9. decided
10. planning

Unit 36
1. taught 2. persuade 3. allow 4. require 5. ordered 6. expect 7. asked 8. warned 9. encouraging
10. reminded

Unit 37
1. kept 2. considered 3. advise 4. risk 5. involves 6. enjoy 7. suggest 8. regret 9. admit 10. avoid

Unit 38
1. on 2. in 3. for, for 4. on 5. for, for 6. about, about 7. to, about 8. with 9. of 10. about

Unit 39
1. of / about 2. from 3. against 4. for 5. for 6. to 7. on 8. on 9. of

Unit 40
1. worth 2. use 3. waste 4. worth 5. point 6. waste 7. point 8. use

Unit 41
1. made 2. makes 3. let 4. let 5. make, make 6. make 7. makes 8. make 9. let 10. let 11. Make,
make

Unit 42
1. some, any 2. any 3. any, some, some 4. any 5. any 6. any (or some) 7. any 8. some 9. any
10. some

Unit 43
1. many 2. much 3. many 4. much, much 5. a lot of 6. a lot of 7. much 8. many 9. much
10. many (or a lot of)

Unit 44
1. a little 2. a few 3. a little 4. a few 5. a few 6. a little 7. a little 8. a few 9. a little
10. a little, a few

Unit 45
1. something, nobody 2. nothing, nothing, nothing, nothing 3. everybody 4. Everybody, nobody 5. anywhere 6. anything 7. something 8. NOBODY, ANYTHING, ANYTHING 9. Anywhere 10. nobody

Unit 46
1. luggage 2. traffic 3. progress 4. information 5. Advice 6. furniture 7. scenery 8. weather

Unit 47
1. my 2. your, ours 3. its 4. his 5. yours 6. her 7. their, your 8. my, yours, Mine 9. their 10. his

Unit 48
1. himself 2. themselves 3. herself 4. myself 5. himself 6. yourself 7. myself 8. yourself 9. ourselves
10. myself

Unit 49
1. depressed, depressing 2. astonishing, astonished 3. shocked, shocking 4. embarrassed, embarrassing
5. annoying, annoyed 6. disappointing, disappointed 7. irritating, irritated 8. amazing, amazing, amazed

Unit 50
1. of, of 2. with / by 3. of 4. at 5. with 6. of 7. about 8. with 9. in 10. with

Unit 51
1. good 2. polite 3. pleased 4. glad 5. relieved 6. sorry 7. shocked 8. important

Unit 52
1. too hot 2. long enough 3. too expensive 4. old enough 5. rich enough 6. too young 7. too short
8. clever enough 9. too big 10. too quick

Unit 53
1. slowly 2. fluently 3. thoroughly 4. accurately 5. instantly 6. fast 7. atrociously 8. well 9. perfectly,
firmly 10. politely, dismissively

Unit 54
1. always 2. often 3. sometimes 4. never 5. usually 6. never 7. never, always 8. always
9. usually 10. always

Unit 55
1. big blue dead 2. nice young intelligent 3. thick English library 4. small black plastic 5. horrible little
brown 6. fast red Italian – £2000 silk evening 7. delicious, home-made chocolate 8. expensive Spanish
acoustic

Unit 56

1. lighter, longer   2. more beautiful   3. faster   4. bigger   5. more intelligent   6. cheaper   7. further   8. older

Unit 57

1. hard   2. high   3. big   4. strong   5. hot   6. long   7. far   8. beautiful   9. fast   10. safe

as black as night, as light as a feather, as old as the hills, as white as snow (or as a sheet), as good as gold, as green as grass, as cold as ice, as free as a bird

Unit 58

1. the quickest   2. the most delicious   3. The easiest   4. the most common   5. the largest   6. the smallest   7. the oldest   8. the best   9. the longest   10. the laziest

Unit 59

1. a cup of tea   2. the letter 'T'   3. lightning   4. a new man   5. a hawk   6. an idiot   7. stars   8. one of the family   9. a glove   10. a pullover

fought like a lion, walks like (a duck, an ape, a monkey), ate like a pig, drinks like a fish

Unit 60

1. who married his sister   2. who interrupts this trial   3. that's advertised outside   4. who was driving the car   5. which contains all the vowels   6. who cut my hair last time I was here   7. that has flat feet, a large hump and is found in Alaska   8. who put his false teeth in backwards   9. that you gave me for my headache   10. who can't stop buying small carpets

Unit 61

1. who was a noisy, spoilt child   2. which I think is the answer to the problem of waste disposal   3. who he thought he recognised   4. which lays square eggs   5. who is 3 metres tall, who is only one metre tall   6. which was pulling a man on water skis across a lake   7. who was sitting next to him

Unit 62

1. wearing   2. made   3. living   4. swimming   5. talking   6. playing, hypnotised   7. lying   8. eating, excited

Unit 63

1. anything you ask for   2. Dr Frankenstein has crossed an ostrich with a centipede   3. you buried your grandmother yesterday   4. you can't swim yet   5. your son needs glasses   6. the cat ate your dinner   7. you've taken an interest in the goldfish   8. I'm still living

Unit 64

1. Because   2. so   3. Because   4. So   5. Because   6. Because   7. so   8. Because   9. so   10. so   11. Because   12. So

Unit 65

1. his feet and legs stayed dry   2. his wig is turning grey   3. hire an octopus to direct traffic   4. oxygen masks to collect nuts   5. they caught fish in their mousetraps   6. his tongue is hanging out   7. the tide refuses to go out   8. the menu and lost my appetite   9. to play tenpin bowling   10. the heat drove me back

Unit 66

1. ears   2. walls   3. feet   4. woman   5. detective   6. eyes   7. mouth   8. town   9. temperatures   10. young man

Unit 67

1. said   2. asked, told   3. told, said   4. asked   5. said   6. asked, said   7. told   8. said

Unit 68

1. how you spell elephant   2. how I can get to the local hospital   3. what vegetarian cannibals eat   4. what the time is   5. where your mother is   6. where the sea is   7. what the chemical formula for water is   8. what kind of insect a slug is

Unit 69

1. didn't you   2. will it   3. didn't I   4. can you, can I   5. aren't you   6. has he   7. is it   8. wouldn't it   9. won't you   10. do you, do I

Unit 70

1. neither   2. So   3. So, Neither   4. either   5. So   6. neither   7. So   8. either   9. So   10. neither

Unit 71

1. he can't talk yet   2. Piggy   3. My name is White   4. I think it's Sitboy   5. Sir Harold   6. she has a heart of stone   7. What's your name?   8. It's Sweetheart

Unit 72

1. in, on   2. between   3. next   4. under, below   5. in, in   6. outside, inside   7. in front   8. on   9. over   10. on   11. on   12. in

Unit 73

1. through   2. over   3. onto   4. down   5. round   6. out of   7. up   8. along   9. under   10. away from

All these verbs can collocate with *through*. Here are some examples: fly through (thick cloud), walk through (a plate glass door), go through (the files), speak through (an interpreter), ride through (the storm), work through (the night), live through (the war), get through (the exam)

Unit 74

1. for   2. with   3. over / about   4. for   5. of   6. for   7. of   8. of   9. for   10. of

Unit 75

1. on   2. in   3. on   4. in   5. for   6. on   7. on   8. at   9. on   10. on

Unit 76

1. before   2. after   3. before   4. before   5. after   6. until   7. after   8. until   9. before   10. until

Unit 77

1. for   2. During   3. while   4. For   5. During   6. for, While   7. during   8. while   9. During   10 while

Unit 78

1. in, out   2. off   3. into   4. down   5. out of   6. up   7. after   8. on   9. up

Unit 79

1. should accidentally fall, should accidentally fall   2. Are you in trouble   3. Let's see what he does with that   4. Sweets   5. A train driver's egg sandwich   6. All of them   7. fell inside   8. Dark, isn't it.   9. Let me see the cup of tea first

ninety eight, ninety nine, a hundred, a hundred and one, a hundred and two

Unit 80

1. cook it on Saturday night   2. get up to answer the telephone   3. had his third birthday   4. finished a march of 31 days   5. I thought you were out   6. just a minute   7. to give you a sleeping pill   8. has gone to your funeral   9. he works at night

Unit 81

1. apple tree is on fire   2. leave the holes on your plate   3. chocolate   4. the smell of its feet   5. have to play inside   6. the woman in the opposite flat   7. my name's Martin   8. Croaka Cola   9. especially at the cinema   10. prefer beef   11. never cleaned one

Unit 82

1. Married   2. full   3. a submarine   4. face   5. pockets   6. a return ticket   7. coffee   8. die   9. soon   10. a new bike